SHAKESPEARE TALES

COMEDIES

Andrew Lynn has a Ph.D. in Renaissance literature from Cambridge University. He now works to help resolve international and cross-border disputes.

www.andrewlynn.com

Shakespeare Tales

Comedies

Charles & Mary Lamb and Harrison Morris

Edited with introductions by Andrew Lynn

HOWGILL
HOUSE

Howgill House Books

www.howgillhousebooks.com

Copyright © Andrew Lynn 2018

ISBN 978-1-912360-09-3

CONTENTS

INTRODUCTION

GENERAL INTRODUCTION

We all want to know Shakespeare.

Of all the great writers, there is none whose influence has spread as far and wide as that of Shakespeare. So profound has been his impact on the culture of the English speaking world, and beyond, that a life lived without some exposure to his work is hard to imagine. To have a passing familiarity with Romeo's passion, Hamlet's introspection, Othello's jealousy, and Lear's rage, is part of the common birthright of humanity. Every one of us is in a position to marvel at Cleopatra's barge burning on the waters of the Nile 'like a burnished throne', to recoil in disgust at Shylock's bloodlust for his 'pound of flesh', to exclaim at Petruchio's 'taming' of his wife through shockingly unmodern methods, to laugh aloud at the love affair between a fairy queen and a bumpkin with a donkey's head one midsummer night near Athens, and to smile darkly at the antics of Richard III seducing a woman whose husband, father,

1

and father-in-law he has all killed at the very funeral procession of the last of those his victims.

That Shakespeare stands at the forefront of world literature has never been seriously disputed. But what is it that almost four centuries after his death continues to draw us back to these works?

For some of us, it is the immensity of Shakespeare's vision and the unparalleled diversity of the worlds he creates and the characters with which he inhabits them. Shakespeare's dramatic journey begins with playful early comedies and thought-provoking histories, passes into a fully-fledged middle period giving rise to profound and disturbing tragedies as well as comedies and histories of a more sophisticated quality, and concludes with his several late romances full of nuance and mystery. We are transported in the comedies to Verona, Padua, Milan, and Messina in Italy, to Ephesus in Greece, to Navarre in northern Spain, and to the quasi-mystical Illyria on the Balkan Peninsula, as well as to the more homely town of Windsor back in England; in the tragedies we journey to the Kingdom of Denmark, the Republic of Venice, the remote Scottish highlands around Inverness, and the castles, heaths, and battlegrounds of ancient Britain; in the classical plays and histories we travel back in time to Rome, Athens, Egypt, and Troy of antiquity, as well as to England of the late Middle Ages; and in the romances we set sail for exotic lands edging the Mediterranean, remote and magical desert islands, and forgotten kingdoms shrouded in the mists of prehistory.

For some of us, on the other hand, what draws us in is the sheer profundity of Shakespeare's work. At every turn, we are confronted with the deep questions of human existence: What is the essence of the human condition? Is there a natural order? What is a man? What is a woman? Our ethics and moral norms are interrogated: What is honour? When must we be loyal and when is it right to rebel? Is it ever right to enact revenge? What are the rewards, if any, of virtue? Political philosophies are cast against each other: monarchism and the divine right of kings meet republicanism and a nascent bourgeois order. Above all, Shakespeare's characters come alive as if born fully formed: overvaunting Macbeth, ludicrous Bottom, introspective Hamlet, melancholic Jacques, treacherous Iago, languorous Cleopatra, and malicious hunchbacked Richard III, among many others, come into being before us with as much vigour as at any time since the turn of the seventeenth century. Shakespeare's contemporary, Ben Jonson, famously said of the Bard: 'He was not of an age, but for all time'. The last 400 years, at least, have tended to bear that contention out.

And for some of us, what makes Shakespeare so compelling is the sheer range and originality of his language. In the first place, there is Shakespeare's legendary vocabulary. Recent studies have taken a more conservative view than those of the past, but even so, Shakespeare's vocabulary of 17,000 to 20,000 words compares favourably to the King James Bible, for example, which makes do with a mere 6,000. But Shakespeare did not just make use of the English language; he also helped to bring it into being. He was a relentless coiner of new words: the Oxford English Dictionary lists 2035 instances where Shakespeare is the first recorded user of a word, compared to about 500 instances for his contemporary, Spencer, 400 for Sidney, and about 50 for the King James Bible. When we say that the 'game is up' (*Cymbeline*) or that 'brevity is the soul of wit' (*Hamlet*); when we see a man 'play fast and loose' (*King John*) or 'hoist with his own petard' (*Hamlet*); when we feel for our 'own flesh and blood' (*The Merchant of Venice*) or are stricken by the 'green-eyed monster' of jealousy (*Othello*); and when we desire 'too much of a good thing' (*As You Like It*) or 'make a virtue of necessity' (*The Two Gentlemen of Verona*)—we are vehicles for Shakespeare's tongue and living testaments to his longevity. Shakespeare breathed life into the language like none other before or since.

To have read and comprehensively understood the thirty-seven plays that Shakespeare is generally accepted to have written would be the work of a lifetime for an industrious scholar. But to know some of the highlights and the broad features of his work is within the reach of all.

The book you now hold in your hands does that by providing classic and elegant prose renditions of

Shakespeare's plays. It is one of a series of five, each focused on a particular genre, which collectively covers the entire Shakespearean dramatic oeuvre: Comedies, Tragedies, Tragicomedies, Roman Tales, and English Histories. By gathering the tales together by genre, we can better appreciate how Shakespeare leads us through several stages of maturation to progressively deepen our experience with the reality he seeks to convey: comedy gives way to the difficulties of tragedy, the ambiguities of tragicomedy, the complexities of history and the bitter-sweet tonalities of romance, much as childhood gives way to adulthood and old age. It is characteristically Shakespearean that his mature vision as expressed in the late plays was neither comic nor tragic but romantic and tragicomic. If there is a final Shakespearean assessment of the human condition, it is that life sends ample measure of both sunshine and showers.

For the most part, the tales provided are the classic nineteenth-century prose versions penned by Charles and Mary Lamb. These versions were intended, in that day and age, to introduce Shakespeare's work to children. This fact should in no way deter the twenty-first-century adult from using them as his or her gateway to the Bard: these versions are adult in style and tone and are totally remote from what we think of today as 'children's literature'. What renders the Lamb versions timeless is their double grace: on the one hand they provide an effortless and pleasurable entry point to the great works of this complex and profound creator, while at the same time preserving, as far as possible, the expressive texture of Shakespeare's own words. The Lambs explain that their versions should not be the end point of the reader's journey: first read the prose tales, they suggest, to obtain a notion of the stories in general; next, explore passages and extracts from the original plays, which stand to be better enjoyed and understood in the light of that general understanding; finally, they suggest, it will be time to turn to the works in full to really experience the 'infinite variety' of Shakespeare's world.

The problem with the Lamb tales is that they are incomplete. Their *Tales from Shakespeare* contains twenty tales of the thirty-seven that we can confidently say Shakespeare wrote. It contains most (but not all) of the comedies: *As You Like It, The Comedy of Errors, A Midsummer Night's Dream, Much Ado About Nothing, The Taming of the Shrew, Twelfth Night*, and *The Two Gentlemen of Verona* are there; *Love's Labour's Lost* and *The Merry Wives of Windsor* are missing. The tragedies are well represented: *Hamlet, King Lear, Macbeth, Othello, Romeo and Juliet*, and *Timon of Athens* are all there. The late romances are also well served: *Cymbeline, Pericles, The Tempest*, and *The Winter's Tale* are all included. But the 'problem plays' are less complete: *All's Well That Ends Well, Measure for Measure*, and *The Merchant of Venice* are included while *Troilus and Cressida* is missing. The

English histories are notable by their complete absence: there is no *King John*; no *Richard II*, *Henry IV*, *Parts 1* or *2*, and no *Henry V*; no *Henry VI*, *Parts 1*, *2* or *3*; no *Richard III*; and no *Henry VIII*. The Roman tales—*Antony and Cleopatra*, *Coriolanus*, and *Julius Caesar*—are nowhere to be found. *Titus Andronicus*—a hybrid that is part tragedy and part Roman play—is also missing.

The Lamb *Tales* need to be supplemented, then, by the works of other Shakespearean scholars and enthusiasts. At the forefront stands the figure of Arthur Quiller-Couch, King Edward VII Professor of English Literature at the University of Cambridge and author in his own right, who published his *Historical Tales from Shakespeare* in the early twentieth century. Quiller-Couch was clear about his mission: he was to put into prose those works ('or most of them') that Charles and Mary Lamb had omitted from their *Tales*. Included in his *Historical Tales* are the near-complete English histories, albeit consolidated by reign so that there are no longer separate 'parts' (King John, Richard II, Henry IV, Henry V, Henry VI, and Richard III), as well as two of the Roman tales (*Coriolanus* and *Julius Caesar*). Quiller-Couch took a slightly different approach from the Lambs: he resolved to tell the tales as simply and straightforwardly as he could in his own manner. The result is, for the most part, a great triumph. Quiller-Couch's evocative narration is the perfect adjunct to the intricate and richly textured fabric of

Shakespearean history. Only one difficulty remained: even the Lamb *Tales* and Quiller-Couch's *Historical Tales* taken together leave us with significant omissions. What has happened to *Love's Labour's Lost* and *The Merry Wives of Windsor*? Why have *Antony and Cleopatra* and *Henry VIII* fallen by the wayside? And where are the two 'deplorables' of the Shakespearean universe—the deeply troubling *Troilus and Cressida* and the unspeakably gruesome *Titus Andronicus*?

To complete the tales, then, we need to cross the pond and turn to Harrison Morris and Winston Stokes. Morris, in his own *Tales from Shakespeare*, almost completes the project. Here we find not only the missing comedies, *Love's Labour's Lost* and *The Merry Wives of Windsor*, but also the hitherto absent *Antony and Cleopatra* and *Henry VIII*, as well as the troublesome *Troilus and Cressida*. Morris' new world sensibilities were not yet ready, however, to expose children to the horrors of *Titus Andronicus*. Only Winston Stokes, in *All Shakespeare's Tales*, was able to screw his courage to the sticking place and pen the prose version of this play. Even Stokes, however, wasn't prepared to communicate Shakespeare in his full Renaissance bloodthirstiness: whereas in Stokes' version Lavinia is 'subjected to cruel tortures', in Shakespeare's original she is raped and has her hands lopped off and tongue cut out; and whereas in Stokes' version Andronicus merely 'makes known' to Tamora that he has killed her sons, in the original play he reveals that he has ground their bones and baked their heads in order to make the very pie she has just been eating.

The striking illustrations that accompany the tales are those of Sir John Gilbert. The product of a more meritocratic age than our own, Gilbert was self-taught and immensely prolific. He illustrated Howard Staunton's three-volume edition of *The Works of Shakespeare*, drawing about twenty illustrations for each play (a total of more than 700 pictures). These illustrations are not inserted simply to decorate the tales; they serve also as wayposts and as aide-mémoires. They bring alive to the eye, as the words do to the ear, the inhabitants and occurrences of Shakespeare's worlds. From Puck and the fairies of *A Midsummer Night's Dream* to the witches of *Macbeth* and the storms and shipwrecks of *Pericles* and *The Tempest*, there is a haunting charm in Gilbert's images that supplements and brings out the magic of the Shakespearean tales.

The *Tales* were intended not simply to engage the intellect, enliven the heart, and lift the spirit. Shakespeare's works were also to be, according to the Lambs, 'enrichers of the fancy, strengtheners of virtue, a withdrawing from all selfish and mercenary thoughts, a lesson of all sweet and honourable thoughts and actions, to teach courtesy, benignity, generosity, humanity'. It has become fashionable among privileged circles to mock the idea that literature can elevate us: the Frankfurt School

Marxist Theodor Adorno has, indeed, famously suggested that 'To write poetry after Auschwitz is barbaric'. And yet that same rejection of the higher capacities of the human soul that is exemplified by Adorno (and those like him) is what has led us to where we are today: demoralized by ugliness, materialism, propaganda, and grinding routine. Our hearts cry out for poetry because we are not bugmen; we are wellsprings of as yet unknown potentialities waiting to be brought to life. Shakespeare, more than any other writer the world has known, by virtue of the tremendous range of experience that he communicates, is able to open us up to a world of possibility. These *Tales* cannot give you that world in its entirety: only the original plays themselves can do that. But they are the entrance point to it. The threshold is right here and right now. Step across.

Introduction to Shakespearean Comedy

Shakespearean comedy is zesty, high-spirited, and powerfully life-affirming. It brims with variety and yet at the same time is always distinctively, uniquely, and characteristically the work of the Bard.

The model for dramatic comedy of the kind written by Shakespeare has come down to us from the Greek New Comedy of Plautus and Terence. What usually happens is this. A young man wants a young woman. His desire is frustrated by opposition which is typically paternal, but may also come from other older males or from some oppressive aspect of society as a whole. Through some twist or device in the plot—which may take place by way of unexpected conversions, miraculous transformations, or providential assistance—the young lovers are brought together and not infrequently married. Comedies are marked by the 'happy ending': a new society forms around the happy couple which is celebrated by a party, banquet, or festive ritual of some kind. While those characters who have played a role blocking or opposing the hero and heroine may be expelled from society at or before this final moment, more often they are included after reconciliation or conversion in a manifestation of 'grace' that is a hallmark of the comic resolution.

Characteristically Shakespearean is the 'romantic

comedy'—a variation on the genre that presents the action moving from the normal world to a festive and forested dream-like 'green world', in which transformations occur and differences are healed, before returning to the normal world bringing back the benefits of what has happened. It is common to look to A Midsummer Night's Dream, written at the height of Shakespeare's comedic powers in the mid-1590s, as an example par excellence of his work in this genre: there we find young lovers subjected to an oppressive marriage law that threatens them with death for following their hearts; we are thrown one midsummer night into the 'green world' of a forest inhabited by fairies and spirits and marked by the effects of magic ointments and spells; we are pulled to-and-fro as the lovers fall in and out of love, subject both to the vicissitudes of that emotion and to the workings of a benevolent, if flawed, supernatural order; we laugh aloud at the well-meaning absurdities of the working men rehearsing a play to impress their superiors; and we rejoice at the miraculous reconciliation of everyone in feasting prior to the blessing by fairies of the respective marriage beds. It is, without doubt, Shakespearean comedy in its purest and most life-affirming form.

There is, however, far more to Shakespearean comedy than that. First in this collection is The Two Gentlemen of Verona, an early romantic comedy in which Shakespeare is perfecting his craft. This is followed by The Taming of the Shrew, in which we

encounter the madcap Petruchio determined to tame
the shrewish Katharine in a tale that displays the
Bard's psychological acuity while at the same time
raising enduring questions about the proper roles and
conduct of men and women. Next up are *The Comedy
of Errors*, a classically inspired work that plays upon
mistaken identity and exposes all that is conventional
and contingent in human nature, and *Love's Labour's
Lost*, in which young men break their oaths to abjure
the company of women only to be schooled in the
truths of love by those self-same women. *A
Midsummer Night's Dream* stands rightly at the centre
of the collection and communicates the basic
polarities of male and female as they play out in the
overlapping worlds of nobles, young lovers, and
fairies. *Much Ado About Nothing* introduces a
threatening undercurrent that arises when men make
'much ado' about female infidelity that never
happened; *As You Like It* follows refugees from court
politics as they learn to find joy, in exile, in what is
right before their eyes. In *The Merry Wives of
Windsor*, one of Shakespeare's most memorable
characters, the fat old rogue Sir John Falstaff from the
Henry IV plays, is given the starring role, on request
(it is said) of Queen Elizabeth, who wished to see him
in love—although in this tale he spends his time
attempting, ludicrously, to seduce suburban
housewives until getting his comeuppance and a good
beating in Windsor Park. The final tale in the
collection, *Twelfth Night*, focusses most insistently on

the question of love: what inspires it, what defeats it, what renders it truly paradoxical, and why—in the end—it will always triumph.

That comedy is light, joyful, and optimistic does not mean that it is without significance. The literary critic, Northrop Frye, has said that the deep structure of comedic action is constituted by a journey from a society controlled by habit, ritual bondage, and arbitrary law at the beginning to a society controlled by youth and pragmatic freedom at the end. To put it more simply, the action of comedy moves from law to liberty; it enacts the gradual de-ossifying and regeneration of a whole society. When we watch or read Shakespeare we do so as individuals but we experience the same potential liberation: with each of his comic tales, Shakespeare invites us too to begin thinking and living differently—with less preconception, less rigidity, and less self-imposed limitation. Whether we accept that invitation is for us to decide.

THE TWO GENTLEMEN OF VERONA

INTRODUCTION

The Two Gentlemen of Verona is one of Shakespeare's earliest works, and one in which we can see him learning his craft. What we have here, say the critics, is Shakespeare making a trial run of the kind of characters we will see developed further in plays such as *Romeo and Juliet*, as well as motifs, such as female characters disguised as male, that we will see again in *As You Like It* and *Twelfth Night*.

The story itself is simple enough. Two gentlemen of Verona, at the outset of the tale, take a different view of love. Proteus is a believer; Valentine a sceptic. Accordingly, when Valentine decides to go abroad to see the wonders of the world, Proteus chooses to stay in Verona with his beloved Julia. When Proteus' father finds out that Valentine has been well received by the Duke of Milan, however, he determines to send Proteus there to join his friend. Valentine in Milan has, meanwhile, fallen in love with the Duke's daughter, Silvia. When Proteus arrives, Valentine discloses his love for Silvia, only for Proteus to decide to pursue her too. When Valentine reveals to Proteus his plan to escape to Mantua with Silvia, then, Proteus decides to betray his friend to the Duke, and having had him exiled proceeds to woo Silvia for himself. Silvia, wooed not only by Proteus but also Thurio, escapes from Milan to join Valentine, is accosted by robbers in a wood, and is rescued by Proteus, who then renews his wooing. It turns out, however, that Valentine now leads this very same band of robbers. Proteus apologizes, Julia reveals that she has been disguised as Proteus' page, and the two pairs of lovers return to Milan to be married before the Duke.

The tale is not without its shocking moments. Most controversial is the scene towards the end of the tale where the reconciliation between the two 'gentlemen' occurs. Valentine, it transpires, hears about the robbers accosting his lady and comes to console her, only to find Proteus once again engaged in 'rudely' pressing her consent to marry. Caught by his friend, however, and 'all at once seized with penitence and remorse', Proteus expresses such a sorrow for the injuries he has done to Valentine, that Valentine not only forgives him, but appears to give up Silvia to him as well: 'I freely do forgive you; and all the interest I have in Silvia, I give it up to you.' While some critics argue that Valentine is merely offering to love Proteus as much as he loves Silvia, there is plainly a more obvious and discomfiting interpretation—namely, that Valentine is literally willing to give up his woman to her 'would-be rapist'.

What are we to make of this?

One answer is to be found in Montaigne's 'On Friendship', which reflects a conventional Renaissance view as to the high esteem in which male-male friendship was to be held:

> To compare this brotherly affection with affection for women . . . it cannot be done; nor can we put the love of women in the same category. Its ardor, I confess . . . is more active, more scorching, and more intense. But it is an impetuous and fickle flame, undulating and variable, a fever flame, subject to fits and lulls, that holds us only by one corner. In friendship it is a general and universal warmth, moderate and even, besides, a constant and settled warmth, with nothing bitter and stinging about it.

Montaigne took a dim view of the capacity of women to achieve the same rarefied connection. 'Besides, to tell the truth, the ordinary capacity of women is inadequate for that communion and fellowship which is the nurse of this sacred bond,' he added, 'nor does their soul seem firm enough to endure the strain of so tight and durable a knot.'[1]

The Two Gentleman of Verona is, then, a Renaissance 'bromance'. Once this is understood, the most curious and perplexing features of the tale begin to make sense. Why should Proteus suddenly begin pursuit of Silvia, when all along he had been infatuated with Julia? The answer may be that he does so because Valentine pursues Silvia, and Proteus is so intimately connected with Valentine, and shares his values and perceptions to such a degree, that pursuit of Silvia would be, in those circumstances, the most natural thing in the world. Likewise, why should Valentine offer his beloved Silvia to Proteus, on the apparently flimsy basis that Proteus has expressed penitence and remorse for wronging Valentine? This only makes sense if the primary value is found in the relationship between the two men, with romantic relationships relegated to an accessory role.

As is so common in Shakespeare's tales, seemingly simple—almost accidental—characters and incidents carry with them profound and subtle shades of meaning. In *The Two Gentleman of Verona*, this subtlety emerges in the figure of Thurio, who provides a revealing contrast to the old world attitudes of Proteus and Valentine. Thurio is Silvia's

---

1. *The Complete Essays of Montaigne*, trans. Donald Frame (Stanford: Stanford University Press, 1957), 137.

authorized suitor: he is the one the Duke of Milan has intended shall marry his daughter. He is, accordingly, under-awed by the antics of Proteus and Valentine. Towards the close of the tale, Thurio asserts his position by attempting to seize Silvia, saying, 'Silvia is mine.' Valentine resists and threatens his death. Thurio draws back, saying that he didn't care for her anyway, and that 'none but a fool would fight for a girl who loved him not.' The Duke of Milan, enraged, retorts that Thurio must be 'base and degenerate' to leave her on 'such slight conditions'. This is the last we hear of Thurio. He is not the hero of the tale, but he heralds the arrival of a more realistic awareness that it is foolish to fight for a woman who does not love you, and that romantic love finds its essence in the meeting of minds rather than extravagant and empty gesture.

THE TWO GENTLEMEN OF VERONA

There lived in the city of Verona two young gentlemen, whose names were Valentine and Proteus, between whom a firm and uninterrupted friendship had long subsisted. They pursued their studies together, and their hours of leisure were always passed in each other's company, except when Proteus visited a lady he was in love with; and these visits to his mistress, and this passion of Proteus for the fair Julia, were the only topics on which these two friends disagreed; for Valentine, not being himself a lover, was sometimes a little weary of hearing his friend forever talking of his Julia, and then he would laugh at Proteus, and in pleasant terms ridicule the passion of love, and declare that no such idle fancies should ever enter his head, greatly preferring (as he said) the free and happy life he led, to the anxious hopes and fears of the lover Proteus.

One morning Valentine came to Proteus to tell him that they must for a time be separated, for that he was going to Milan. Proteus, unwilling to part with his friend, used many arguments to prevail upon Valentine not to leave him; but Valentine said, 'Cease to persuade me, my loving Proteus. I will not, like a sluggard, wear out my youth in idleness at home. Home-keeping youths have ever homely wits. If your affection were not chained to the sweet glances of your honored Julia, I would entreat you to accompany me, to see the wonders of the world abroad; but since you are a lover, love on still, and may your love be prosperous!'

They parted with mutual expressions of unalterable friendship. 'Sweet Valentine, adieu!' said Proteus. 'Think on me, when you see some rare object worthy of notice in your travels, and wish me partaker of your happiness.'

Valentine began his journey that same day towards Milan; and when his friend had left him, Proteus sat down to write a letter to Julia, which he gave to her maid Lucetta to deliver to her mistress.

Julia loved Proteus as well as he did her, but she was a lady of a noble spirit, and she thought it did not become her maiden dignity too easily to be won; therefore she affected to be insensible of his passion, and gave him much uneasiness in the prosecution of his suit.

And when Lucetta offered the letter to Julia, she would not receive it, and chid her maid for taking letters from Proteus, and ordered her to leave the room. But she so much wished to see what was written in the letter, that she soon called in her maid again; and when Lucetta returned, she said: 'What o'clock is it?' Lucetta, who knew her mistress more desired to see the letter than to know the time of day, without answering her question, again offered the rejected letter. Julia, angry that her maid should thus take the liberty of seeming to know what she really wanted, tore the letter in pieces, and threw it on the floor, ordering her maid once more out of the room. As Lucetta was retiring, she stopped to pick up the fragments of the torn letter; but Julia, who meant not so to part with them, said, in pretended anger: 'Go, get you gone, and let the papers lie; you would be fingering them to anger me.'

Julia then began to piece together as well as she could the torn fragments. She first made out these words: 'Love-wounded Proteus'; and lamenting over these and suchlike loving words, which she made out though they were all torn asunder, or, she said wounded (the expression 'Love-wounded Proteus' giving her that idea), she talked to these kind words, telling them she would lodge them in her bosom as in a bed, till their wounds were healed, and that she would kiss each several piece, to make amends.

In this manner she went on talking with a pretty ladylike childishness, till finding herself unable to make out the whole, and vexed at her own ingratitude in destroying such sweet and loving words, as she called them, she wrote a much kinder letter to Proteus than she had ever done before.

Proteus was greatly delighted at receiving this favourable answer to his letter; and while he was reading it, he exclaimed: 'Sweet love, sweet lines, sweet life!'

In the midst of his raptures he was interrupted by his father. 'How now!' said the old gentleman. 'What letter are you reading there?'

'My lord,' replied Proteus, 'it is a letter from my friend Valentine, at Milan.'

'Lend me the letter,' said his father. 'Let me see what news.'

'There are no news, my lord,' said Proteus, greatly alarmed, 'but that he writes how well beloved he is of the Duke of Milan, who daily graces him with favours; and how he wishes me with him, the partner of his fortune.'

'And how stand you affected to his wish?' asked the father.

'As one relying on your lordship's will, and not depending on his friendly wish,' said Proteus.

Now it had happened that Proteus' father had just been talking with a friend on this very subject: his friend had said, he wondered his lordship suffered his son to spend his youth at home, while most men were sending their sons to seek preferment abroad; 'some,' said he, 'to the wars, to try their fortunes there, and some to discover islands far away, and some to study in foreign universities; and there is his companion Valentine, he is gone to the Duke of Milan's court. Your son is fit for any of these things, and it will be a great disadvantage to him in his riper age not to have travelled in his youth.'

Proteus' father thought the advice of his friend was very good, and upon Proteus telling him that Valentine 'wished him with him, the partner of his fortune,' he at once determined to send his son to Milan; and without giving Proteus any reason for this sudden resolution, it being the usual habit of this positive old gentleman to command his son, not reason with him, he said: 'My will is the same as Valentine's wish'; and seeing his son look astonished, he added: 'Look not amazed, that I so suddenly resolve you shall spend some time in the Duke of

Milan's court; for what I will I will, and there is an end. Tomorrow be in readiness to go. Make no excuses; for I am peremptory.'

Proteus knew it was of no use to make objections to his father, who never suffered him to dispute his will; and he blamed himself for telling his father an untruth about Julia's letter, which had brought upon him the sad necessity of leaving her.

Now that Julia found she was going to lose Proteus for so long a time, she no longer pretended indifference; and they bade each other a mournful farewell, with many vows of love and constancy. Proteus and Julia exchanged rings, which they both promised to keep forever in remembrance of each other; and thus, taking a sorrowful leave, Proteus set out on his journey to Milan, the abode of his friend Valentine.

Valentine was in reality what Proteus had feigned

to his father, in high favour with the Duke of Milan; and another event had happened to him, of which Proteus did not even dream, for Valentine had given up the freedom of which he used so much to boast, and was become as passionate a lover as Proteus.

She who had wrought this wondrous change in Valentine was the lady Silvia, daughter of the Duke of Milan, and she also loved him; but they concealed their love from the Duke, because although he showed much kindness for Valentine, and invited him every day to his palace, yet he designed to marry his daughter to a young courtier whose name was Thurio. Silvia despised this Thurio, for he had none of the fine sense and excellent qualities of Valentine.

These two rivals, Thurio and Valentine, were one day on a visit to Silvia, and Valentine was entertaining Silvia with turning everything Thurio said into ridicule, when the Duke himself entered the room, and told Valentine the welcome news of his friend Proteus' arrival. Valentine said: 'If I had wished a thing, it would have been to have seen him here!' And then he highly praised Proteus to the Duke, saying: 'My lord, though I have been a truant of my time, yet hath my friend made use and fair advantage of his days, and is complete in person and in mind, in all good grace to grace a gentleman.'

'Welcome him then according to his worth,' said the Duke. 'Silvia, I speak to you, and you, Sir Thurio; for Valentine, I need not bid him do so.' They were here interrupted by the entrance of Proteus, and

Valentine introduced him to Silvia, saying: 'Sweet lady, entertain him to be my fellow-servant to your ladyship.'

When Valentine and Proteus had ended their visit, and were alone together, Valentine said: 'Now tell me how all does from whence you came? How does your lady, and how thrives your love?' Proteus replied: 'My tales of love used to weary you. I know you joy not in a love discourse.'

'Ay, Proteus,' returned Valentine, 'but that life is altered now. I have done penance for condemning love. For in revenge of my contempt of love, love has chased sleep from my enthralled eyes. O gentle Proteus, Love is a mighty lord, and hath so humbled me, that I confess there is no woe like his correction, nor no such joy on earth as in his service. I now like no discourse except it be of love. Now I can break my fast, dine, sup, and sleep, upon the very name of love.'

This acknowledgement of the change which love had made in the disposition of Valentine was a great triumph to his friend Proteus. But 'friend' Proteus must be called no longer, for the same all-powerful deity Love, of whom they were speaking (yea, even while they were talking of the change he had made in Valentine), was working in the heart of Proteus; and he, who had till this time been a pattern of true love and perfect friendship, was now, in one short interview with Silvia, become a false friend and a faithless lover; for at the first sight of Silvia all his love for Julia vanished away like a dream, nor did his long friendship for Valentine deter him from endeavouring to supplant him in her affections; and although, as it will always be, when people of dispositions naturally good become unjust, he had many scruples before he determined to forsake Julia, and become the rival of Valentine; yet he at length overcame his sense of duty, and yielded himself up, almost without remorse, to his new unhappy passion.

Valentine imparted to him in confidence the whole history of his love, and how carefully they had concealed it from the Duke her father, and told him, that, despairing of ever being able to obtain his consent, he had prevailed upon Silvia to leave her father's palace that night, and go with him to Mantua; then he showed Proteus a ladder of ropes, by help of which he meant to assist Silvia to get out of one of the windows of the palace after it was dark.

Upon hearing this faithful recital of his friend's dearest secrets, it is hardly possible to be believed, but so it was, that Proteus resolved to go to the Duke, and disclose the whole to him.

This false friend began his tale with many artful speeches to the Duke, such as that by the laws of friendship he ought to conceal what he was going to reveal, but that the gracious favour the Duke had shown him, and the duty he owed his grace, urged him to tell that which else no worldly good should draw from him. He then told all he had heard from Valentine, not omitting the ladder of ropes, and the manner in which Valentine meant to conceal them under a long cloak.

The Duke thought Proteus quite a miracle of integrity, in that he preferred telling his friend's intention rather than he would conceal an unjust action, highly commended him, and promised him not to let Valentine know from whom he had learnt this intelligence, but by some artifice to make Valentine betray the secret himself. For this purpose the Duke awaited the coming of Valentine in the evening, whom he soon saw hurrying towards the palace, and he perceived somewhat was wrapped within his cloak, which he concluded was the rope-ladder.

The Duke upon this stopped him, saying: 'Whither away so fast, Valentine?' 'May it please your grace,' said Valentine, 'there is a messenger that stays to bear my letters to my friends, and I am going to deliver them.' Now this falsehood of Valentine's had no better success in the event than the untruth Proteus told his father.

'Be they of much import?' said the Duke.

'No more, my lord,' said Valentine, 'than to tell my father I am well and happy at your grace's court.'

'Nay then,' said the Duke, 'no matter; stay with me a while. I wish your counsel about some affairs that concern me nearly.' He then told Valentine an artful story, as a prelude to draw his secret from him, saying that Valentine knew he wished to match his daughter with Thurio, but that she was stubborn and disobedient to his commands, 'neither regarding,' said he, 'that she is my child, nor fearing me as if I were her father. And I may say to thee, this pride of hers has drawn my love from her. I had thought my age should have been cherished by her childlike duty. I now am resolved to take a wife, and turn her out to whosoever will take her in. Let her beauty be her wedding dower, for me and my possessions she esteems not.'

Valentine, wondering where all this would end, made answer: 'And what would your grace have me do in all this?'

'Why,' said the Duke, 'the lady I would wish to marry is nice and coy, and does not much esteem my aged eloquence. Besides, the fashion of courtship is much changed since I was young; now I would willingly have you to be my tutor to instruct me how I am to woo.'

Valentine gave him a general idea of the modes of courtship then practised by young men, when they wished to win a fair lady's love, such as presents, frequent visits, and the like.

The Duke replied to this, that the lady did refuse a present which he sent her, and that she was so strictly kept by her father, that no man might have access to her by day.

'Why then,' said Valentine, you must visit her by night.'

'But at night,' said the artful Duke, who was now coming to the drift of his discourse, 'her doors are fast locked.'

Valentine then unfortunately proposed that the Duke should go into the lady's chamber at night by means of a ladder of ropes, saying he would procure him one fitting for that purpose; and in conclusion advised him to conceal this ladder of ropes under such a cloak as that which he now wore. 'Lend me your cloak,' said the Duke, who had feigned this long story on purpose to have a pretence to get off the cloak; so upon saying these words, he caught hold of Valentine's cloak, and throwing it back, he discovered not only the ladder of ropes, but also a letter of Silvia's, which he instantly opened and read; and this letter contained a full account of their intended elopement. The Duke, after upbraiding Valentine for his ingratitude in thus returning the favour he had shown him by endeavouring to steal away his daughter, banished him from the court and city of Milan forever; and Valentine was forced to depart that night, without even seeing Silvia.

While Proteus at Milan was thus injuring Valentine, Julia at Verona was regretting the absence of Proteus; and her regard for him at last so far overcame her sense of propriety, that she resolved to leave Verona, and seek her lover at Milan; and to secure herself from danger on the road, she dressed her maiden Lucetta and herself in men's clothes, and they set out in this disguise, and arrived at Milan soon after Valentine was banished from that city through the treachery of Proteus.

Julia entered Milan about noon, and she took up her abode at an inn; and her thoughts being all on her dear Proteus, she entered into conversation with the innkeeper, or host, as he was called, thinking by that means to learn some news of Proteus.

The host was greatly pleased that this handsome young gentleman (as he took her to be), who from his appearance he concluded was of high rank, spoke so familiarly to him; and being a good-natured man, he was sorry to see him look so melancholy; and to amuse his young guest, he offered to take him to hear some fine music, with which, he said, a gentleman that evening was going to serenade his mistress.

The reason Julia looked so very melancholy was that she did not well know what Proteus would think of the imprudent step she had taken; for she knew he had loved her for her noble maiden pride and dignity of character, and she feared she should lower herself in his esteem; and this it was that made her wear a sad and thoughtful countenance.

She gladly accepted the offer of the host to go with him, and hear the music; for she secretly hoped she might meet Proteus by the way.

But when she came to the palace whither the host conducted her, a very different effect was produced to what the kind host intended; for there, to her heart's sorrow, she beheld her lover, the inconstant Proteus, serenading the lady Silvia with music, and addressing discourse of love and admiration to her. And Julia overheard Silvia from a window talk with Proteus, and reproach him for forsaking his own true lady, and for his ingratitude to his friend Valentine; and then Silvia left the window, not choosing to listen to his music and his fine speeches; for she was a faithful lady to her banished Valentine, and abhorred the ungenerous conduct of his false friend Proteus.

Though Julia was in despair at what she had just witnessed, yet did she still love the truant Proteus; and hearing that he had lately parted with a servant, she contrived with the assistance of her host, the friendly innkeeper, to hire herself to Proteus as a page; and Proteus knew not she was Julia, and he sent her with letters and presents to her rival Silvia, and he even sent by her the very ring she gave him as a parting gift at Verona.

When she went to that lady with the ring, she was

most glad to find that Silvia utterly rejected the suit of Proteus; and Julia, or the page Sebastian as she was called, entered into conversation with Silvia about Proteus' first love, the forsaken lady Julia. She putting in (as one may say) a good word for herself, said she knew Julia; as well she might, being herself the Julia of whom she spoke; telling how fondly Julia loved her master Proteus, and how his unkind neglect would grieve her; and then she with a pretty equivocation went on: 'Julia is about my height, and of my complexion, the colour of her eyes and hair the same as mine'; and indeed Julia looked a most beautiful youth in her boy's attire. Silvia was moved to pity this lovely lady, who was so sadly forsaken by the man she loved; and when Julia offered the ring which Proteus had sent, refused it, saying: 'The more shame for him that he sends me that ring; I will not take it; for I have often heard him say his Julia gave it to him. I love thee, gentle youth, for pitying her, poor lady! Here is a purse; I give it you for Julia's sake.' These comfortable words coming from her kind rival's tongue cheered the drooping heart of the disguised lady.

But to return to the banished Valentine; who scarce knew which way to bend his course, being unwilling to return home to his father a disgraced and banished man: as he was wandering over a lonely forest, not far distant from Milan, where he had left his heart's dear treasure, the lady Silvia, he was set upon by robbers, who demanded his money.

Valentine told them that he was a man crossed by adversity, that he was going into banishment, and that he had no money, the clothes he had on being all his riches.

The robbers, hearing that he was a distressed man, and being struck with his noble air and manly behaviour, told him if he would live with them, and be their chief, or captain, they would put themselves under his command; but that if he refused to accept their offer, they would kill him.

Valentine, who cared little what became of himself, said he would consent to live with them and be their captain, provided they did no outrage on women or poor passengers.

Thus the noble Valentine became, like Robin Hood, of whom we read in ballads, a captain of robbers and outlawed banditti; and in this situation he was found by Silvia, and in this manner it came to pass.

Silvia, to avoid a marriage with Thurio, whom her father insisted upon her no longer refusing, came at last to the resolution of following Valentine to Mantua, at which place she had heard her lover had taken refuge; but in this account she was misinformed, for he still lived in the forest among the robbers, bearing the name of their captain, but taking no part in their depredations, and using the authority which they had imposed upon him in no other way than to compel them to show compassion to the travellers they robbed.

Silvia contrived to effect her escape from her

father's palace in company with a worthy old gentleman, whose name was Eglamour, whom she took along with her for protection on the road.

She had to pass through the forest where Valentine and the banditti dwelt; and one of these robbers seized on Silvia, and would also have taken Eglamour, but he escaped.

The robber who had taken Silvia, seeing the terror she was in, bid her not be alarmed, for that he was only going to carry her to a cave where his captain lived, and that she need not be afraid, for their captain had an honourable mind, and always showed humanity to women. Silvia found little comfort in hearing she was going to be carried as a prisoner before the captain of a lawless banditti. 'O Valentine,' she cried, 'this I endure for thee!'

But as the robber was conveying her to the cave of his captain, he was stopped by Proteus, who, still attended by Julia in the disguise of a page, having heard of the flight of Silvia, had traced her steps to this forest. Proteus now rescued her from the hands of the robber; but scarce had she time to thank him for the service he had done her, before he began to distress her afresh with his love suit; and while he was rudely pressing her to consent to marry him, and his page (the forlorn Julia) was standing beside him in great anxiety of mind, fearing lest the great service which Proteus had just done to Silvia should win her to show him some favour, they were all strangely surprised with the sudden appearance of Valentine, who, having heard his robbers had taken a lady prisoner, came to console and relieve her.

Proteus was courting Silvia, and he was so much ashamed of being caught by his friend, that he was all at once seized with penitence and remorse; and he expressed such a lively sorrow for the injuries he had done to Valentine, that Valentine, whose nature was noble and generous, even to a romantic degree, not only forgave and restored him to his former place in his friendship, but in a sudden flight of heroism he said: 'I freely do forgive you; and all the interest I have in Silvia, I give it up to you.' Julia, who was standing beside her master as a page, hearing this strange offer, and fearing Proteus would not be able with this new-found virtue to refuse Silvia, fainted, and they were all employed in recovering her: else would Silvia have been offended at being thus made over to Proteus, though she could scarcely think that Valentine would long persevere in this overstrained and too generous act of friendship. When Julia recovered from the fainting fit, she said: 'I had forgot, my master ordered me to deliver this ring to Silvia.' Proteus, looking upon the ring, saw that it was the one he gave to Julia, in return for that which he received from her, and which he had sent by the supposed page to Silvia. 'How is this?' said he, 'this is Julia's ring: how came you by it, boy?' Julia answered: 'Julia herself did give it me, and Julia herself hath brought it hither.'

Proteus, now looking earnestly upon her, plainly perceived that the page Sebastian was no other than the lady Julia herself; and the proof she had given of her constancy and true love so wrought in him, that his love for her returned into his heart, and he took again his own dear lady, and joyfully resigned all pretensions to the lady Silvia to Valentine, who had so well deserved her.

Proteus and Valentine were expressing their happiness in their reconciliation, and in the love of their faithful ladies when they were surprised with the sight of the Duke of Milan and Thurio, who came there in pursuit of Silvia.

Thurio first approached, and attempted to seize Silvia, saying: 'Silvia is mine.' Upon this Valentine said to him in a very spirited manner: 'Thurio, keep back: if once again you say that Silvia is yours, you shall embrace your death. Here she stands, take but possession of her with a torch! I dare you but to breathe upon my love.' Hearing this threat, Thurio, who was a great coward, drew back, and said he cared not for her, and that none but a fool would fight for a girl who loved him not.

The Duke, who was a very brave man himself, said now in great anger: 'The more base and degenerate in you to take such means for her as you have done, and leave her on such slight conditions.' Then turning to Valentine, he said: 'I do applaud your spirit, Valentine, and think you worthy of an empress's love. You shall have Silvia, for you have well deserved her.' Valentine then with great humility kissed the Duke's hand, and accepted the noble present which he had made him of his daughter with becoming thankfulness; taking occasion of this joyful minute to entreat the goodhumoured Duke to pardon the thieves with whom he had associated in the forest, assuring him, that when reformed and restored to society, there would be found among them many good, and fit for great employment; for the most of them had been banished, like Valentine, for state offences, rather than for any black crimes they had been guilty of.

To this the ready Duke consented; and now nothing remained but that Proteus, the false friend, was ordained, by way of penance for his love-prompted faults, to be present at the recital of the whole story of his loves and falsehoods before the Duke; and the shame of the recital to his awakened conscience was judged sufficient punishment; which being done, the lovers, all four, returned back to Milan, and their nuptials were solemnized in the presence of the Duke, with high triumphs and feasting.

41

2

THE TAMING OF
THE SHREW

INTRODUCTION

The Taming of the Shrew is a humorous account of one
man's successful efforts to bring his woman into a
state of dutiful obedience.

The story proper begins when Petruchio, a bold
and high-tempered gentleman, arrives in Padua in
search of a rich wife. He soon learns of a wealthy
gentleman of Padua by the name of Baptista who has
two unmarried daughters. The youngest, Bianca, is
gentle and demure, and has several suitors. The
eldest, Katharine, on the other hand, is a 'shrew': she
is a wild, fiery-tempered, and ungovernable scold.
Baptista has, however, determined not to agree to
Bianca marrying until Katharine is off his hands.
Undeterred, Petruchio resolves to take the shrewish

43

Katharine as his wife, and boldly sets about wooing her. He goes about the task of taming this shrew with confidence and gusto: he is late for and disrupts the wedding, takes her to his home only to raise endless objections to simple requests for food and clothing, and steadfastly refuses to cooperate with her until she sees things his way. By the time Petruchio and Katharine return to her father's home to celebrate Bianca's wedding, Katharine has been comprehensively 'tamed', a fact that is proved at the wedding feast when three wives are tested for obedience to their husbands—and only Katharine comes good.

Much of the tale's interest comes from the uninhibited perspective it takes on the age-old 'war of the sexes': it is a story about men and women and their respective roles. But it is also a story about the methods by which one person may exert influence—in this case, compelling influence—over another.

The first method is 'reframing'. Frames, according to cognitive scientists, are mental structures that shape the way we see the world—our goals, actions, values, and sense of reality. Reframing is what occurs when a person is able to adjust another person's frame so that they see the world differently afterwards. From the outset, Petruchio refuses to take Katharine at her own estimation; she insists on being called, formally, Katharine, but Petruchio has none of it: 'You lie,' he says to her abruptly, 'for you are called plain Kate, and bonny Kate, and sometimes Kate the Shrew.' This advances Petruchio's objectives in that it reframes Katherine as someone not totally able to impose her own subjective self-concept on the world. But the tale also shows that this is not all bad for Katharine either. Where conventional society had limited her by defining her as a shrew, Petruchio's wooing opens her up to new ways of thinking about herself: 'If she rails at me, why then I will tell her she sings as sweetly as a nightingale; and if she frowns, I will say she looks as clear as roses newly washed with dew.'

The second method is what Shakespeare calls 'killing by kindness'. This is a pun. The 'kindness' here refers both to Petruchio's unbearably solicitous attention to Katharine's needs—an attention so extreme that Katharine is herself eventually driven to reject it—as well as Petruchio's adopting the same 'kind' of excessive and unreasonable behaviour as Katharine. Petruchio's genius is in knowing that there is no prospect of persuading Katharine by argument. Instead, he makes her understand experientially that she does not really want what she thinks she wants (i.e. to have her every whim catered for). Rather than insisting, from the outside, upon the behaviour he desires from her, he makes her want to make that change herself.

Finally, Petruchio insists upon bringing Katharine into his own reality. He looks at the sun and calls it the moon—and requires Katharine to agree. He then calls it the sun—and also requires Katharine to agree. Katharine is finally overcome when she is totally willing to accept Petruchio's reality, however absurd. Of course, the relabelling of sun as moon and moon as sun is extreme. Nevertheless, the scene reflects the more pervasive truth that human experience is inevitably tinged with subjective factors, and it is when our subjective reality dovetails with the subjective reality of another that we really have the foundation for a stable partnership.

Petruchio's approach is not one that would be approved of today. But is it necessary to totally reject the message of the tale? In Franco Zeffirelli's gorgeous 1967 cinematic version of the play, Elizabeth Taylor's Katharine is frequently shown smiling to herself after Richard Burton's Petruchio has taken his steps to 'tame' her: here at least she plainly takes pleasure in testing the wherewithal of the man who seeks to take her as a wife. The battle of the sexes is not, however, one to be continued ad nauseam. It is, at best, a prelude to the harnessing of two strong souls in a shared reality without which domestic peace is unlikely to be obtained.

THE TAMING OF THE SHREW

Katharine, the Shrew, was the eldest daughter of Baptista, a rich gentleman of Padua. She was a lady of such an ungovernable spirit and fiery temper, such a loud-tongued scold, that she was known in Padua by no other name than Katharine the Shrew. It seemed very unlikely, indeed impossible, that any gentleman would ever be found who would venture to marry this lady, and therefore Baptista was much blamed for deferring his consent to many excellent offers that were made to her gentle sister Bianca, putting off all Bianca's suitors with this excuse, that when the eldest sister was fairly off his hands they should have free leave to address young Bianca.

It happened, however, that a gentleman, named Petruchio, came to Padua purposely to look out for a wife, who, nothing discouraged by these reports of Katharine's temper, and hearing she was rich and handsome, resolved upon marrying this famous termagant, and taming her into a meek and manageable wife. And truly none was so fit to set about this herculean labour as Petruchio, whose spirit was as high as Katharine's, and he was a witty and most happy-tempered humorist, and withal so wise, and of such a true judgement, that he well knew how to feign a passionate and furious deportment, when his spirits were so calm that himself could have laughed merrily at his own angry feigning, for his natural temper was careless and easy; the boisterous airs he assumed when he became the husband of Katharine being but in sport, or more properly speaking, affected by his excellent discernment, as the only means to overcome, in her own way, the passionate ways of the furious Katharine.

A courting then Petruchio went to Katharine the Shrew; and first of all he applied to Baptista her father, for leave to woo his gentle daughter Katharine, as Petruchio called her, saying archly, that having heard of her bashful modesty and mild behaviour, he had come from Verona to solicit her love. Her father, though he wished her married, was forced to confess Katharine would ill answer this character, it being soon apparent of what manner of gentleness she was composed, for her music-master rushed into the room to complain that the gentle Katharine, his pupil, had broken his head with her lute for presuming to find fault with her performance; which, when Petruchio heard, he said: 'It is a brave wench; I love her more than ever, and long to have some chat with her'; and hurrying the old gentleman for a positive answer, he said: 'My business is in haste, signior Baptista, I cannot come every day to woo. You knew my father: he is dead, and has left me heir to all his lands and goods. Then tell me, if I get your daughter's love, what dowry you will give with her.' Baptista thought his manner was somewhat blunt for a lover; but being glad to get Katharine married, he answered that he would give her twenty thousand crowns for her dowry, and half his estate at his death: so this odd match was quickly agreed on, and Baptista went to apprise his shrewish daughter of her lover's addresses, and sent her in to Petruchio to listen to his suit.

In the meantime Petruchio was settling with himself the mode of courtship he should pursue; and he said: 'I will woo her with some spirit when she comes. If she rails at me, why then I will tell her she sings as sweetly as a nightingale; and if she frowns, I will say she looks as clear as roses newly washed with dew. If she will not speak a word, I will praise the eloquence of her language; and if she bids me leave her, I will give her thanks as if she bid me stay with her a week.' Now the stately Katharine entered, and Petruchio first addressed her with 'Good morrow, Kate, for that is your name, I hear.' Katharine, not liking this plain salutation, said disdainfully: 'They call me Katharine who do speak to me.' 'You lie,' replied the lover, 'for you are called plain Kate, and bonny Kate, and sometimes Kate the Shrew; but, Kate, you are the prettiest Kate in Christendom, and therefore, Kate, hearing your mildness praised in every town, I am come to woo you for my wife.'

A strange courtship they made of it. She in loud and angry terms showing him how justly she had gained the name of Shrew, while he still praised her sweet and courteous words, till at length, hearing her father coming, he said (intending to make as quick a wooing as possible): 'Sweet Katharine, let us set this idle chat aside, for your father has consented that you shall be my wife, your dowry is agreed on, and whether you will or no, I will marry you.' And now Baptista entering, Petruchio told him his daughter had received him kindly, and that she had promised to be married the next Sunday. This Katharine denied, saying she would rather see him hanged on Sunday, and reproached her father for wishing to wed her to such a madcap ruffian as Petruchio. Petruchio desired her father not to regard her angry words, for they had agreed she should seem reluctant before him, but that when they were alone he had found her very fond and loving; and he said to her: 'Give me your hand, Kate; I will go to Venice to buy you fine apparel against our wedding day. Provide the feast, father, and bid the wedding guests. I will be sure to bring rings, fine array, and rich clothes, that my Katharine may be fine; and kiss me, Kate, for we will be married on Sunday.'

On the Sunday all the wedding guests were assembled, but they waited long before Petruchio came, and Katharine wept for vexation to think that Petruchio had only been making a jest of her. At last, however, he appeared; but he brought none of the bridal finery he had promised Katharine, nor was he dressed himself like a bridegroom, but in strange disordered attire, as if he meant to make a sport of the serious business he came about; and his servant and the very horses on which they rode were in like manner in mean and fantastic fashion habited.

Petruchio could not be persuaded to change his dress; he said Katharine was to be married to him, and not to his clothes; and finding it was in vain to argue with him, to the church they went, he still behaving in the same mad way, for when the priest asked Petruchio if Katharine should be his wife, he swore so loud that she should, that, all amazed, the priest let fall his book, and as he stooped to take it up, this mad-brained bridegroom gave him such a cuff that down fell the priest and his book again. And all the while they were being married he stamped and swore so, that the high spirited Katharine trembled and shook with fear. After the ceremony was over, while they were yet in the church, he called for wine, and drank a loud health to the company, and threw a sop which was at the bottom of the glass full in the sexton's face, giving no other reason for this strange act than that the sexton's beard grew thin and hungerly, and seemed to ask the sop as he was drinking. Never sure was there such a mad marriage; but Petruchio did but put this wildness on, the better to succeed in the plot he had formed to tame his shrewish wife.

Baptista had provided a sumptuous marriage feast, but when they returned from church, Petruchio, taking hold of Katharine, declared his intention of carrying his wife home instantly; and no remonstrance of his father-in-law, or angry words of the enraged Katharine, could make him change his purpose. He claimed a husband's right to dispose of his wife as he pleased, and away he hurried Katharine off: he seeming so daring and resolute that no one dared attempt to stop him.

Petruchio mounted his wife upon a miserable horse, lean and lank, which he had picked out for the purpose, and himself and his servant no better mounted; they journeyed on through rough and miry ways, and ever when this horse of Katharine's stumbled, he would storm and swear at the poor jaded beast, who could scarce crawl under his burthen, as if he had been the most passionate man alive.

At length, after a weary journey, during which Katharine had heard nothing but the wild ravings of Petruchio at the servant and the horses, they arrived at his house. Petruchio welcomed her kindly to her home, but he resolved she should have neither rest nor food that night. The tables were spread, and supper soon served; but Petruchio, pretending to find fault with every dish, threw the meat about the floor, and ordered the servants to remove it away; and all this he did, as he said, in love for his Katharine, that she might not eat meat that was not well dressed. And when Katharine, weary and supperless, retired to rest, he found the same fault with the bed, throwing the pillows and bedclothes about the room, so that she was forced to sit down in a chair, where if she chanced to drop asleep, she was presently awakened by the loud voice of her husband, storming at the servants for the ill-making of his wife's bridal bed.

The next day Petruchio pursued the same course, still speaking kind words to Katharine, but when she attempted to eat, finding fault with everything that was set before her, throwing the breakfast on the floor as he had done the supper; and Katharine, the haughty Katharine, was fain to beg the servants would bring her secretly a morsel of food; but they being instructed by Petruchio, replied, they dared not give her anything unknown to their master. 'Ah,' said she, 'did he marry me to famish me? Beggars that come to my father's door have food given them. But I, who never knew what it was to entreat for anything, am starved for want of food, giddy for want of sleep, with oaths kept waking, and with brawling fed; and that which vexes me more than all, he does it under the name of perfect love, pretending that if I sleep or eat, it were present death to me.' Here the soliloquy was interrupted by the entrance of Petruchio: he, not meaning she should be quite starved, had brought her a small portion of meat, and he said to her: 'How fares my sweet Kate? Here, love, you see how diligent I am, I have dressed your meat myself. I am sure this kindness merits thanks. What, not a word? Nay, then you love not the meat, and all the pains I have taken is to no purpose.' He then ordered the servant to take the dish away. Extreme hunger, which had abated the pride of Katharine, made her say, though angered to the heart: 'I pray you let it stand.' But this was not all Petruchio intended to bring her to, and he replied: 'The poorest service is repaid with thanks, and so shall mine before you touch the meat.' On this Katharine brought out a reluctant 'I thank you, sir.' And now he suffered her to make a slender meal, saying: 'Much good may it do your gentle heart, Kate; eat apace! And now, my honey love, we will return to your father's house, and revel it as bravely as the best, with silken coats and caps and golden rings, with ruffs and scarfs and fans and double change of finery'; and to make her believe he really intended to give her these gay things, he called in a tailor and a haberdasher, who brought some new clothes he had ordered for her, and then giving her plate to the servant to take away, before she had half satisfied her hunger, he said: 'What, have you dined?'

The haberdasher presented a cap, saying: 'Here is the cap your worship bespoke'; on which Petruchio began to storm afresh, saying the cap was moulded in a porringer, and that it was no bigger than a cockle or walnut shell, desiring the haberdasher to take it away and make it bigger. Katharine said: 'I will have this; all gentlewomen wear such caps as these.' 'When you are gentle,' replied Petruchio, 'you shall have one too, and not till then.'

The meat Katharine had eaten had a little revived her fallen spirits, and she said: 'Why, sir, I trust I may have leave to speak, and speak I will: I am no child, no babe; your betters have endured to hear me say my mind; and if you cannot, you had better stop your ears.' Petruchio would not hear these angry words, for he had happily discovered a better way of managing his wife than keeping up a jangling argument with her; therefore his answer was: 'Why, you say true; it is a paltry cap, and I love you for not liking it.' 'Love me, or love me not,' said Katharine, 'I like the cap, and I will have this cap or none.' 'You say you wish to see the gown,' said Petruchio, still affecting to misunderstand her. The tailor then came forward and showed her a fine gown he had made for her. Petruchio, whose intent was that she should have neither cap nor gown, found as much fault with that. 'O mercy, Heaven!' said he, 'what stuff is here! What, do you call this a sleeve? It is like a demi-cannon, carved up and down like an apple tart.' The tailor said: 'You bid me make it according to the fashion of the times'; and Katharine said, she never saw a better fashioned gown. This was enough for Petruchio, and privately desiring these people might be paid for their goods, and excuses made to them for the seemingly strange treatment he bestowed upon them, he with fierce words and furious gestures drove the tailor and the haberdasher out of the room; and then, turning to Katharine, he said: 'Well, come, my Kate, we will go to your father's even in these mean garments we now wear.'

And then he ordered his horses, affirming they should reach Baptista's house by dinnertime, for that it was but seven o'clock. Now it was not early morning, but the very middle of the day, when he spoke this; therefore Katharine ventured to say, though modestly, being almost overcome by the vehemence of his manner: 'I dare assure you, sir, it is two o'clock, and will be suppertime before we get there.' But Petruchio meant that she should be so completely subdued that she should assent to everything he said, before he carried her to her father; and therefore, as if he were lord even of the sun, and could command the hours, he said it should be what time he pleased to have it, before he set forward: 'For,' he said, 'whatever I say or do, you still are crossing it. I will not go to-day, and when I go, it shall be what o'clock I say it is.' Another day Katharine was forced to practise her newly found obedience, and not till he had brought her proud spirit to such a perfect subjection, that she dared not remember there was

such a word as contradiction, would Petruchio allow
her to go to her father's house; and even while they
were upon their journey thither, she was in danger of
being turned back again, only because she happened
to hint it was the sun, when he affirmed the moon
shone brightly at noonday. 'Now, by my mother's
son,' said he, 'and that is myself, it shall be the moon,
or stars, or what I list, before I journey to your father's
house.' He then made as if he were going back again;
but Katharine, no longer Katharine the Shrew, but
the obedient wife, said: 'Let us go forward, I pray,
now we have come so far, and it shall be the sun, or
moon, or what you please, and if you please to call it
a rush candle henceforth, I vowed it shall be so for
me.' This he was resolved to prove, therefore he said
again: 'I say, it is the moon.' 'I know it is the moon,'
replied Katharine. 'You lie, it is the blessed sun,' said
Petruchio. 'Then it is the blessed sun,' replied
Katharine; 'but sun it is not, when you say it is not.
What you will have it named, even so it is, and so
it ever shall be for Katharine.' Now then he suffered
her to proceed on her journey; but further to try if
this yielding humour would last, he addressed an old
gentleman they met on the road as if he had been a
young woman, saying to him: 'Good morrow, gentle
mistress'; and asked Katharine if she had ever beheld
a fairer gentlewoman, praising the red and white of
the old man's cheeks, and comparing his eyes to two
bright stars; and again he addressed him, saying: 'Fair
lovely maid, once more good day to you!' and said to

his wife: 'Sweet Kate, embrace her for her beauty's sake.' The now completely vanquished Katharine quickly adopted her husband's opinion, and made her speech in like sort to the old gentleman, saying to him: 'Young budding virgin, you are fair, and fresh, and sweet: whither are you going, and where is your dwelling? Happy are the parents of so fair a child.' 'Why, how now, Kate,' said Petruchio, 'I hope you are not mad. This is a man, old and wrinkled, faded and withered, and not a maiden, as you say he is.' On this Katharine said: 'Pardon me, old gentleman; the sun has so dazzled my eyes, that everything I look on seemeth green. Now I perceive you are a reverend father: I hope you will pardon me for my sad mistake.' 'Do, good old grandsire,' said Petruchio, 'and tell us which way you are travelling. We shall be glad of your good company, if you are going our way.' The old gentleman replied: 'Fair sir, and you my merry mistress, your strange encounter has much amazed me. My name is Vincentio, and I am going to visit a son of mine who lives at Padua.' Then Petruchio knew the old gentleman to be the father of Lucentio, a young gentleman who was to be married to Baptista's younger daughter, Bianca, and he made Vincentio very happy by telling him the rich marriage his son was about to make; and they all journeyed on pleasantly together till they came to Baptista's house, where there was a large company assembled to celebrate the wedding of Bianca and Lucentio,

Baptista having willingly consented to the marriage of Bianca when he had got Katharine off his hands.

When they entered, Baptista welcomed them to the wedding feast, and there was present also another newly married pair.

Lucentio, Bianca's husband, and Hortensio, the other new married man, could not forbear sly jests, which seemed to hint at the shrewish disposition of Petruchio's wife, and these fond bridegrooms seemed high pleased with the mild tempers of the ladies they had chosen, laughing at Petruchio for his less fortunate choice. Petruchio took little notice of their jokes till the ladies were retired after dinner, and then he perceived Baptista himself joined in the laugh against him; for when Petruchio affirmed that his wife would prove more obedient than theirs, the father of Katharine said: 'Now, in good sadness, son Petruchio, I fear you have got the veriest shrew of all.' 'Well,' said

Petruchio, 'I say no, and therefore for assurance that I speak the truth, let us each one send for his wife, and he whose wife is most obedient to come at first when she is sent for shall win a wager which we will propose.' To this the other two husbands willingly consented, for they were quite confident that their gentle wives would prove more obedient than the headstrong Katharine; and they proposed a wager of twenty crowns, but Petruchio merrily said, he would lay as much as that upon his hawk or hound, but twenty times as much upon his wife. Lucentio and Hortensio raised the wager to a hundred crowns, and Lucentio first sent his servant to desire Bianca would come to him. But the servant returned, and said: 'Sir, my mistress sends you word she is busy and cannot come.' 'How,' said Petruchio, 'does she say she is busy and cannot come? Is that an answer for a wife?' Then they laughed at him, and said it would be well if Katharine did not send him a worse answer. And now it was Hortensio's turn to send for his wife; and he said to his servant: 'Go, and entreat my wife to come to me.' 'Oh ho! Entreat her!' said Petruchio. 'Nay, then, she needs must come.' 'I am afraid, sir,' said Hortensio, 'your wife will not be entreated.' But presently this civil husband looked a little blank, when the servant returned without his mistress; and he said to him: 'How now! Where is my wife?' 'Sir,' said the servant, 'my mistress says you have some goodly jest in hand, and therefore she will not come. She bids you come to her.' 'Worse and worse!' said

Petruchio; and then he sent his servant, saying: 'Sirrah, go to your mistress, and tell her I command her to come to me.' The company had scarcely time to think she would not obey this summons, when Baptista, all in amaze, exclaimed: 'Now, by my holidame, here comes Katharine!' And she entered, saying meekly to Petruchio: 'What is your will, sir, that you send for me?' 'Where is your sister and Hortensio's wife?' said he. Katharine replied: 'They sit conferring by the parlour fire.' 'Go, fetch them hither!' said Petruchio. Away went Katharine without reply to perform her husband's command. 'Here is a wonder,' said Lucentio, 'if you talk of a wonder.' 'And so it is,' said Hortensio. 'I marvel what it bodes.' 'Marry, peace it bodes,' said Petruchio, 'and love, and quiet life, and right supremacy; and, to be short, everything that is sweet and happy.' Katharine's father, overjoyed to see this reformation in his daughter, said: 'Now, fair befall thee, son Petruchio! You have won the wager, and I will add another twenty thousand crowns to her dowry, as if she were another daughter, for she is changed as if she had never been.' 'Nay,' said Petruchio, 'I will win the wager better yet, and show more signs of her newbuilt virtue and obedience.' Katharine now entering with the two ladies, he continued: 'See where she comes, and brings your froward wives as prisoners to her womanly persuasion. Katharine, that cap of yours does not become you; off with that bauble, and throw it under foot.' Katharine instantly took off her cap, and threw it down. 'Lord!' said Hortensio's wife. 'May I never have a cause to sigh till I am brought to such a silly pass!' And Bianca, she too said: 'Fie, what foolish duty call you this?' On this Bianca's husband said to her: 'I wish your duty were as foolish too! The wisdom of your duty, fair Bianca, has cost me a hundred crowns since dinnertime.' 'The more fool you,' said Bianca, 'for laying on my duty.' 'Katharine,' said Petruchio, 'I charge you tell these headstrong women what duty they owe their lords and husbands.' And to the wonder of all present, the reformed shrewish lady spoke as eloquently in praise of the wife-like duty of obedience as she had practised it implicitly in a ready submission to Petruchio's will. And Katharine once more became famous in Padua, not as heretofore, as Katharine the Shrew, but as Katharine the most obedient and duteous wife in Padua.

3

THE COMEDY OF ERRORS

INTRODUCTION

The Comedy of Errors is one of Shakespeare's earliest works. Based on the *Menaechmi* by the Roman dramatist, Plautus, it's a short but masterful tale of the reunion of long-lost family members after years of separation.

It begins with the discovery of a wanderer from Syracuse, an old merchant by the name of Aegeon, in the streets of the ancient Greek city of Ephesus. By landing there, Aegeon has broken a law that provides for any merchant from Syracuse to be put to death unless he can pay a thousand-mark ransom. Brought before the Duke of Ephesus, Aegeon explains how he long ago lost his wife and the elder of his twin sons in a shipwreck, and then lost his younger son too, who had set out in search of them. In fact, although Aegeon has no knowledge of it, his twin sons are both in Ephesus, unbeknownst to each other, as are their twin servants. After a series of encounters in which the twins are mistaken for each other, leading to wrongful beatings, near seduction, alleged infidelity, and false accusations of theft and madness, the family members are reunited and Aegeon pardoned.

The driving force behind the tale is the human desire to be 'completed' through others. Aegeon has lost his wife and sons and naturally desires to be reunited with them. The younger son for his part is driven by a need to reunite with his elder twin brother. The shrewish wife of the elder brother, Adriana, clings to and harries him due to an obsessive desire to protect the relationship and the meaning it gives to her. Even the servants are affected by this drive to completion through others, each of them on their reunion being 'well pleased to see his own person (as in a glass) show so handsome in his brother'.

The Comedy of Errors presents with great vividness the difficulty of establishing personal identity in the absence of recognized social relationships. Each of the twin brothers, being mistaken for the other, is thrown into a whirlwind of confusion. On the one hand, the younger twin inadvertently steps into the role of the elder, and benefits from his accrued social capital including the ministrations of a wife and the services of craftsmen; conversely, the elder brother is effectively stripped of what is due to him by virtue of his long-term role in his society. The tale shows how a substantial part of our personhood arises from the relational equity and social capital we have accumulated; to be deprived of that, or to have another's attributed to us, is to lose an essential part of what it is to be 'us'. Moreover, our actions only make sense in their social context: the exact same conduct of the twin brothers appears as madness or even demonic possession when each has stepped into the role of the other.

It is characteristically Shakespearean, nevertheless, to acknowledge that there will always be an irreducible core of personhood that exists above and beyond social ties. In *The Comedy of Errors*, it is Emilia who has cultivated this personal core most completely: she has retreated into a life of religious contemplation as abbess of a priory at Ephesus, having been shipwrecked and separated from both her husband and sons many years earlier, where she resides in quiet dignity awaiting with equanimity whatever life holds in store for her. We are not *fully* ourselves without our network of social relationships, suggests Shakespeare. But we are, equally, not *truly* ourselves unless there is also part of us that remains inviolable and forever beyond the power of fortune to disturb.

THE COMEDY OF ERRORS

The states of Syracuse and Ephesus being at variance, there was a cruel law made at Ephesus, ordaining that if any merchant of Syracuse was seen in the city of Ephesus, he was to be put to death, unless he could pay a thousand marks for the ransom of his life.

Aegeon, an old merchant of Syracuse, was discovered in the streets of Ephesus, and brought before the Duke, either to pay this heavy fine, or to receive sentence of death.

Aegeon had no money to pay the fine, and the Duke, before he pronounced the sentence of death upon him, desired him to relate the history of his life, and to tell for what cause he had ventured to come to the city of Ephesus, which it was death for any Syracusan merchant to enter.

Aegeon said that he did not fear to die, for sorrow had made him weary of his life, but that a heavier task could not have been imposed upon him than to relate the events of his unfortunate life. He then began his own history, in the following words:

'I was born at Syracuse, and brought up to the profession of a merchant. I married a lady, with whom I lived very happily, but being obliged to go to Epidamnum, I was detained there by my business six months, and then, finding I should be obliged to stay some time longer, I sent for my wife, who, as soon as she arrived, was brought to bed of two sons, and what was very strange, they were both so exactly alike, that it was impossible to distinguish the one from the other. At the same time that my wife was brought to bed of these twin boys, a poor woman in the inn where my wife lodged was brought to bed of two sons, and these twins were as much like each other as my two sons were. The parents of these children being exceeding poor, I bought the two boys, and brought them up to attend upon my sons.

'My sons were very fine children, and my wife was not a little proud of two such boys; and she daily wishing to return home, I unwillingly agreed, and in an evil hour we got on shipboard; for we had not sailed above a league from Epidamnum before a dreadful storm arose, which continued with such violence, that the sailors seeing no chance of saving the ship, crowded into the boat to save their own lives, leaving us alone in the ship, which we every moment expected would be destroyed by the fury of the storm.

'The incessant weeping of my wife, and the piteous complaints of the pretty babes, who, not knowing what to fear, wept for fashion, because they saw their mother weep, filled me with terror for them, though I did not for myself fear death; and all my thoughts were bent to contrive means for their safety. I tied my youngest son to the end of a small spare mast, such as seafaring men provide against storms; at the other end I bound the youngest of the twin slaves, and at the same time I directed my wife how to fasten the other children in like manner to another mast. She thus having the care of the two eldest children, and I of the two younger, we bound ourselves separately to these masts with the children; and but for this contrivance we had all been lost, for the ship split on a mighty rock, and was dashed in pieces; and we, clinging to these slender masts, were supported above the water, where I, having the care of two children, was unable to assist my wife, who with the other children was soon separated from me; but while they were yet in my sight, they were taken up by a boat of fishermen, from Corinth (as I supposed), and seeing them in safety, I had no care but to struggle with the wild sea-waves, to preserve my dear son and the youngest slave. At length we, in our turn, were taken up by a ship, and the sailors, knowing me, gave us kind welcome and assistance, and landed us in safety at Syracuse; but from that sad hour I have never known what became of my wife and eldest child.

'My youngest son, and now my only care, when he was eighteen years of age, began to be inquisitive after his mother and his brother, and often importuned me that he might take his attendant, the young slave, who had also lost his brother, and go in search of them: at length I unwillingly gave consent, for though I anxiously desired to hear tidings of my wife and eldest son, yet in sending my younger one to find them, I hazarded the loss of them also. It is now seven years since my son left me; five years have I passed in travelling through the world in search of him: I have been in farthest Greece, and through the bounds of Asia, and coasting homewards, I landed here in Ephesus, being unwilling to leave any place unsought that harbours men; but this day must end the story of my life, and happy should I think myself in my death, if I were assured my wife and sons were living.'

Here the hapless Aegeon ended the account of his misfortunes; and the Duke, pitying this unfortunate father, who had brought upon himself this great peril by his love for his lost son, said, if it were not against the laws, which his oath and dignity did not permit him to alter, he would freely pardon him; yet, instead of dooming him to instant death, as the strict letter of the law required, he would give him that day to try if he could beg or borrow the money to pay the fine.

This day of grace did seem no great favour to Aegeon, for not knowing any man in Ephesus, there seemed to him but little chance that any stranger would lend or give him a thousand marks to pay the fine; and helpless and hopeless of any relief, he retired from the presence of the Duke in the custody of a jailor.

Aegeon supposed he knew no person in Ephesus; but at the very time he was in danger of losing his life through the careful search he was making after his youngest son, that son and his eldest son also were both in the city of Ephesus.

Aegeon's sons, besides being exactly alike in face and person, were both named alike, being both called Antipholus, and the two twin slaves were also both named Dromio. Aegeon's youngest son, Antipholus of Syracuse, he whom the old man had come to Ephesus to seek, happened to arrive at Ephesus with his slave Dromio that very same day that Aegeon did; and he being also a merchant of Syracuse, he would have been in the same danger that his father was, but by good fortune he met a friend who told him the peril an old merchant of Syracuse was in, and advised him to pass for a merchant of Epidamnum; this Antipholus agreed to do, and he was sorry to hear one of his own countrymen was in this danger, but he little thought this old merchant was his own father.

The eldest son of Aegeon (who must be called Antipholus of Ephesus, to distinguish him from his brother Antipholus of Syracuse) had lived at Ephesus twenty years, and, being a rich man, was well able to have paid the money for the ransom of his father's life; but Antipholus knew nothing of his father, being so young when he was taken out of the sea with his mother by the fishermen that he only remembered he had been so preserved, but he had no recollection of either his father or his mother; the fishermen who took up this Antipholus and his mother and the young slave Dromio, having carried the two children away from her (to the great grief of that unhappy lady), intending to sell them.

Antipholus and Dromio were sold by them to Duke Menaphon, a famous warrior, who was uncle to the Duke of Ephesus, and he carried the boys to Ephesus when he went to visit the Duke his nephew.

The Duke of Ephesus taking a liking to young Antipholus, when he grew up, made him an officer in his army, in which he distinguished himself by his great bravery in the wars, where he saved the life of his patron the Duke, who rewarded his merit by marrying him to Adriana, a rich lady of Ephesus; with whom he was living (his slave Dromio still attending him) at the time his father came there.

Antipholus of Syracuse, when he parted with his friend, who advised him to say he came from Epidamnum, gave his slave Dromio some money to carry to the inn where he intended to dine, and in the meantime he said he would walk about and view the city, and observe the manners of the people.

Dromio was a pleasant fellow, and when Antipholus was dull and melancholy he used to divert himself with the odd humours and merry jests of his slave, so that the freedoms of speech he allowed in Dromio were greater than is usual between masters and their servants.

When Antipholus of Syracuse had sent Dromio away, he stood awhile thinking over his solitary wanderings in search of his mother and his brother, of whom in no place where he landed could he hear the least tidings; and he said sorrowfully to himself. 'I am like a drop of water in the ocean, which seeking to find its fellow drop, loses itself in the wide sea. So I unhappily, to find a mother and a brother, do lose myself'

While he was thus meditating on his weary travels, which had hitherto been so useless, Dromio (as he thought) returned. Antipholus, wondering that he came back so soon, asked him where he had left the money. Now it was not his own Dromio, but the twin brother that lived with Antipholus of Ephesus, that he spoke to. The two Dromios and the two Antipholuses were still as much alike as Aegeon had said they were in their infancy; therefore no wonder Antipholus thought it was his own slave returned, and asked him why he came back so soon. Dromio replied: 'My mistress sent me to bid you come to dinner. The capon burns and the pig falls from the spit, and the meat will be all cold if you do not come home.' 'These jests are out of season,' said Antipholus. 'Where did you leave the money?' Dromio still answering that his mistress had sent him to fetch Antipholus to dinner: 'What mistress?' said Antipholus. 'Why, your worship's wife, sir,' replied Dromio. Antipholus having no wife, he was very angry with Dromio, and said: 'Because I familiarly sometimes chat with you, you presume to jest with me in this free manner. I am not in a sportive humour now: where is the money? We being strangers here, how dare you trust so great a charge from your own custody?' Dromio hearing his master, as he thought him, talk of their being strangers supposing Antipholus was jesting, replied merrily: 'I pray you, sir, jest as you sit at dinner. I had no charge but to fetch you home, to dine with my mistress and her sister.' Now Antipholus lost all patience, and beat Dromio, who ran home, and told his mistress that his master had refused to come to dinner, and said that he had no wife.

Adriana, the wife of Antipholus of Ephesus, was very angry when she heard that her husband said he had no wife; for she was of a jealous temper, and she said her husband meant that he loved another lady better than herself; and she began to fret, and say unkind words of jealousy and reproach of her husband; and her sister Luciana, who lived with her, tried in vain to persuade her out of her groundless suspicions.

Antipholus of Syracuse went to the inn, and found Dromio with the money in safety there, and seeing his own Dromio, he was going again to chide him for his free jests, when Adriana came up to him, and not doubting but it was her husband she saw, she began to reproach him for looking strange upon her (as well he might, never having seen this angry lady before); and then she told him how well he loved her before they were married, and that now he loved some other lady instead of her. 'How comes it now, my husband,' said she, 'O how comes it that I have lost your love?' 'Plead you to me, fair dame?' said the astonished Antipholus.

It was in vain he told her he was not her husband,

and that he had been in Ephesus but two hours; she insisted on his going home with her, and Antipholus at last, being unable to get away, went with her to his brother's house, and dined with Adriana and her sister, the one calling him husband, and the other brother, he, all amazed, thinking he must have been married to her in his sleep, or that he was sleeping now. And Dromio, who followed them, was no less surprised, for the cook-maid, who was his brother's wife, also claimed him for her husband.

While Antipholus of Syracuse was dining with his brother's wife, his brother, the real husband, returned home to dinner with his slave Dromio; but the servants would not open the door, because their mistress had ordered them not to admit any company; and when they repeatedly knocked, and said they were Antipholus and Dromio, the maids laughed at them, and said that Antipholus was at dinner with their mistress, and Dromio was in the kitchen; and though they almost knocked the door down, they could not gain admittance, and at last Antipholus went away very angry, and strangely surprised at hearing a gentleman was dining with his wife.

When Antipholus of Syracuse had finished his dinner, he was so perplexed at the lady's still persisting in calling him husband, and at hearing that Dromio had also been claimed by the cook-maid, that he left the house as soon as he could find any pretence to get away; for though he was very much pleased with Luciana, the sister, yet the jealous-tempered Adriana he disliked very much, nor was Dromio at all better satisfied with his fair wife in the kitchen; therefore both master and man were glad to get away from their new wives as fast as they could.

The moment Antipholus of Syracuse had left the house, he was met by a goldsmith, who mistaking him, as Adriana had done, for Antipholus of Ephesus, gave him a gold chain, calling him by his name; and when Antipholus would have refused the chain, saying it did not belong to him, the goldsmith replied he made it by his own orders; and went away, leaving the chain in the hands of Antipholus, who ordered his man Dromio to get his things on board a ship, not choosing to stay in a place any longer where he met with such strange adventures that he surely thought himself bewitched.

The goldsmith who had given the chain to the wrong Antipholus was arrested immediately after for a sum of money he owed; and Antipholus, the married brother, to whom the goldsmith thought he had given the chain, happened to come to the place where the officer was arresting the goldsmith, who, when he saw Antipholus, asked him to pay for the gold chain he had just delivered to him, the price amounting to nearly the same sum as that for which he had been arrested. Antipholus denying the having received the chain, and the goldsmith persisting to declare that he had but a few minutes before given it to him, they disputed this matter a long time, both thinking they were right: for Antipholus knew the goldsmith never gave him the chain, and so like were the two brothers, the goldsmith was as certain he had delivered the chain into his hands, till at last the officer took the goldsmith away to prison for the debt he owed, and at the same time the goldsmith made the officer arrest Antipholus for the price of the chain; so that at the conclusion of their dispute, Antipholus and the merchant were both taken away to prison together.

As Antipholus was going to prison, he met Dromio of Syracuse, his brother's slave, and mistaking him for his own, he ordered him to go to Adriana his wife, and tell her to send the money for which he was arrested. Dromio wondering that his master should send him back to the strange house where he dined, and from which he had just before been in such haste to depart, did not dare to reply, though he came to tell his master the ship was ready to sail: for he saw Antipholus was in no humour to be jested with. Therefore he went away, grumbling within himself, that he must return to Adriana's house, 'Where,' said he, 'Dowsabel claims me for a husband: but I must go, for servants must obey their masters' commands.'

Adriana gave him the money, and as Dromio was returning, he met Antipholus of Syracuse, who was still in amaze at the surprising adventures he met with; for his brother being well known in Ephesus, there was hardly a man he met in the streets but saluted him as an old acquaintance: some offered him money which they said was owing to him, some invited him to come and see them, and some gave thanks for kindnesses they said he had done them, all mistaking him for his brother. A tailor showed him some silks he had bought for him, and insisted upon taking measure of him for some clothes.

Antipholus began to think he was among a nation of sorcerers and witches, and Dromio did not at all relieve his master from his bewildered thoughts, by asking him how he got free from the officer who was carrying him to prison, and giving him the purse of gold which Adriana had sent to pay the debt with. This talk of Dromio's of the arrest and of a prison, and of the money he had brought from Adriana, perfectly confounded Antipholus, and he said: 'This fellow Dromio is certainly distracted, and we wander here in illusions'; and quite terrified at his own confused thoughts, he cried out: 'Some blessed power deliver us from this strange place!'

And now another stranger came up to him, and she was a lady, and she too called him Antipholus, and told him he had dined with her that day, and asked him for a gold chain which she said he had promised to give her. Antipholus now lost all patience, and calling her a sorceress, he denied that he had ever promised her a chain, or dined with her, or had ever seen her face before that moment. The lady persisted in affirming he had dined with her, and had promised her a chain, which Antipholus still denying, she further said that she had given him a valuable ring, and if he would not give her the gold chain, she insisted upon having her own ring again. On this Antipholus became quite frantic, and again calling her sorceress and witch, and denying all knowledge of her or her ring, ran away from her, leaving her astonished at his words and his wild looks, for nothing to her appeared more certain than that he had dined with her, and that she had given him a ring, in consequence of his promising to make her a present of a gold chain. But this lady had fallen into the same mistake the others had done, for she had taken him for his brother: the married Antipholus had done all the things she taxed this Antipholus with.

When the married Antipholus was denied entrance into his own house (those within supposing him to be already there), he had gone away very angry, believing it to be one of his wife's jealous freaks, to which she was very subject, and remembering that she had often falsely accused him of visiting other ladies, he, to be revenged on her for shutting him out of his own house determined to go and dine with this lady, and she receiving him with great civility, and his wife having so highly offended him, Antipholus promised to give her a gold chain, which he had intended as a present for his wife; it was the same chain which the goldsmith by mistake had given to his brother. The lady liked so well the thoughts of having a fine gold chain, that she gave the married Antipholus a ring; which when, as she supposed (taking his brother for him), he denied, and said he did not know her, and left her in such a wild passion, she began to think he was certainly out of his senses; and presently she resolved to go and tell Adriana that her husband was mad. And while she was telling it to Adriana, he came, attended by the jailor (who allowed him to come home to get the money to pay the debt), for the purse of money, which Adriana had sent by Dromio, and he had delivered to the other Antipholus.

Adriana believed the story the lady told her of her husband's madness must be true, when he reproached her for shutting him out of his own house; and remembering how he had protested all dinnertime that he was not her husband, and had never been in Ephesus till that day, she had no doubt that he was mad; she therefore paid the jailor the money, and having discharged him, she ordered her servants to bind her husband with ropes, and had him conveyed into a dark room, and sent for a doctor to come and cure him of his madness: Antipholus all the while hotly exclaiming against this false accusation, which the exact likeness he bore to his brother had brought upon him. But his rage only the more confirmed them in the belief that he was mad; and Dromio persisting in the same story, they bound him also, and took him away along with his master.

Soon after Adriana had put her husband into confinement, a servant came to tell her that Antipholus and Dromio must have broken loose from their keepers, for that they were both walking at liberty in the next street. On hearing this, Adriana ran out to fetch him home, taking some people with her to secure her husband again; and her sister went along with her. When they came to the gates of a convent in their neighbourhood, there they saw Antipholus and Dromio, as they thought, being again deceived by the likeness of the twin brothers.

Antipholus of Syracuse was still beset with the perplexities this likeness had brought upon him. The chain which the goldsmith had given him was about his neck, and the goldsmith was reproaching him for denying that he had it, and refusing to pay for it, and Antipholus was protesting that the goldsmith freely gave him the chain in the morning, and that from that hour he had never seen the goldsmith again.

And now Adriana came up to him and claimed him as her lunatic husband, who had escaped from his keepers; and the men she brought with her were going to lay violent hands on Antipholus and

Dromio; but they ran into the convent, and Antipholus begged the abbess to give him shelter in her house.

And now came out the lady abbess herself to inquire into the cause of this disturbance. She was a grave and venerable lady, and wise to judge of what she saw, and she would not too hastily give up the man who had sought protection in her house; so she strictly questioned the wife about the story she told of her husband's madness, and she said: 'What is the cause of this sudden distemper of your husband's? Has he lost his wealth at sea? Or is it the death of some dear friend that has disturbed his mind?' Adriana replied, that no such things as these had been the cause. 'Perhaps,' said the abbess, 'he has fixed his affections on some other lady than you his wife; and that has driven him to this state.' Adriana said she had long thought the love of some other lady was the cause of his frequent absences from home. Now it was not his love for another, but the teasing jealousy of his wife's temper, that often obliged Antipholus to leave his home; and (the abbess suspecting this from the vehemence of Adriana's manner) to learn the truth, she said: 'You should have reprehended him for this.' 'Why, so I did,' replied Adriana. 'Ay,' said the abbess, 'but perhaps not enough.' Adriana, willing to convince the abbess that she had said enough to Antipholus on this subject, replied: 'It was the constant subject of our conversation: in bed I would not let him sleep for speaking of it. At table I would

86

not let him eat for speaking of it. When I was alone with him, I talked of nothing else; and in company I gave him frequent hints of it. Still all my talk was how vile and bad it was in him to love any lady better than me.'

The lady abbess, having drawn this full confession from the jealous Adriana, now said: 'And therefore comes it that your husband is mad. The venomous clamour of a jealous woman is a more deadly poison than a mad dog's tooth. It seems his sleep was hindered by your railing: no wonder that his head is light; and his meat was sauced with your upbraidings; unquiet meals make ill digestions, and that has thrown him into this fever. You say his sports were disturbed by your brawls; being debarred from the enjoyment of society and recreation, what could ensue but dull melancholy and comfortless despair? The consequence is, then, that your jealous fits have made your husband mad.'

Luciana would have excused her sister, saying she always reprehended her husband mildly; and she said to her sister: 'Why do you hear these rebukes without answering them?' But the abbess had made her so plainly perceive her fault, that she could only answer: 'She has betrayed me to my own reproof.'

Adriana, though ashamed of her own conduct, still insisted on having her husband delivered up to her; but the abbess would suffer no person to enter her house, nor would she deliver up this unhappy man to the care of the jealous wife, determining herself to use gentle means for his recovery, and she retired into her house again, and ordered her gates to be shut against them.

During the course of this eventful day, in which so many errors had happened from the likeness the twin brothers bore to each other, old Aegeon's day of grace was passing away, it being now near sunset; and at sunset he was doomed to die, if he could not pay the money.

The place of his execution was near this convent, and here he arrived just as the abbess retired into the convent; the Duke attending in person, that if any offered to pay the money, he might be present to pardon him.

Adriana stopped this melancholy procession, and cried out to the Duke for justice, telling him that the abbess had refused to deliver up her lunatic husband to her care.

While she was speaking, her real husband and his servant Dromio, who had got loose, came before the Duke to demand justice, complaining that his wife had confined him on a false charge of lunacy; and telling in what manner he had broken his bands, and eluded the vigilance of his keepers. Adriana was strangely surprised to see her husband, when she thought he had been within the convent.

Aegeon, seeing his son, concluded this was the son who had left him to go in search of his mother and his brother; and he felt secure that his dear son would readily pay the money demanded for his ransom. He therefore spoke to Antipholus in words of fatherly affection, with joyful hope that he should now be released. But to the utter astonishment of Aegeon, his son denied all knowledge of him, as well he might, for this Antipholus had never seen his father since they were separated in the storm in his infancy; but while the poor old Aegeon was in vain endeavouring to make his son acknowledge him, thinking surely that either his griefs and the anxieties he had suffered had so strangely altered him that his son did not know him, or else that he was ashamed to acknowledge his father in his misery; in the midst of this perplexity, the lady abbess and the other Antipholus and Dromio came out and the wondering Adriana saw two husbands and two Dromios standing before her.

And now these riddling errors, which had so perplexed them all, were clearly made out. When the Duke saw the two Antipholuses and the two Dromios

89

both so exactly alike, he at once conjectured aright of these seeming mysteries, for he remembered the story Aegeon had told him in the morning; and he said, these men must be the two sons of Aegeon and their twin slaves.

But now an unlooked-for joy indeed completed the history of Aegeon; and the tale he had in the morning told in sorrow, and under sentence of death, before the setting sun went down was brought to a happy conclusion, for the venerable lady abbess made herself known to be the long-lost wife of Aegeon, and the fond mother of the two Antipholuses.

When the fishermen took the eldest Antipholus and Dromio away from her, she entered a nunnery, and by her wise and virtuous conduct, she was at length made lady abbess of this convent, and in discharging the rites of hospitality to an unhappy stranger she had unknowingly protected her own son.

Joyful congratulations and affectionate greetings between these long separated parents and their children made them for a while forget that Aegeon was yet under sentence of death; but when they were become a little calm, Antipholus of Ephesus offered the Duke the ransom money for his father's life; but the Duke freely pardoned Aegeon, and would not take the money. And the Duke went with the abbess and her newly found husband and children into the convent to hear this happy family discourse at leisure of the blessed ending of their adverse fortunes. And the two Dromios' humble joy must not be forgotten;

they had their congratulations and greetings too, and each Dromio pleasantly complimented his brother on his good looks, being well pleased to see his own person (as in a glass) show so handsome in his brother.

Adriana had so well profited by the good counsel of her mother-in-law, that she never after cherished unjust suspicions, or was jealous of her husband.

Antipholus of Syracuse married the fair Luciana, the sister of his brother's wife; and the good old Aegeon, with his wife and sons, lived at Ephesus many years. Nor did the unravelling of these perplexities so entirely remove every ground of mistake for the future, but that sometimes, to remind them of adventures past, comical blunders would happen, and the one Antipholus, and the one Dromio, be mistaken for the other, making altogether a pleasant and diverting Comedy of Errors.

4

LOVE'S LABOUR'S LOST

Introduction

Love's Labour's Lost is focussed on the way we conduct our amorous relationships. Poking fun at both excessive idolatry as well as sexual hypocrisy, it closes on an unexpectedly mournful note, suggesting that love is matured and enriched by an awareness of the inevitability of death.

The setting of the tale is the Kingdom of Navarre in what is now a part of northern Spain. The King of Navarre and his friends, the Lords Biron, Longaville, and Dumain, decide to devote themselves to a contemplative life of study for three years, abjuring all contact with women for that period. Despite Biron's reservations, the men accordingly swear an oath to that effect. Difficulties arise when shortly thereafter the Princess of France arrives on embassy from her father regarding the surrender to him of the territory of Aquitaine, bringing three ladies—Rosaline, Maria, and Katharine—in her train. The King, so as not to break his oath, detains the Princess and her ladies in a field outside the court while the matter is resolved. However, he begins to fall in love with the Princess, and his Lords Biron, Longaville, and Dumain proceed to fall in love with Rosaline, Maria, and Katharine respectively. When the men become aware of each others' oath-breaking, they quickly find a way of justifying their conduct to themselves, and resolve to approach the ladies in the guise of Russians to test their affections. The ladies, having been forewarned of the plan, decide to mock the courtiers by disguising themselves as each other. The King and his courtiers are exposed, but before they can make amends for their foolery, news is brought from France of the death of the Princess' father. The Princess swears she will be the King of Navarre's wife but only if he retreats to a hermitage to spend a year in austerity, remote from the pleasures of the world. Similar terms are imposed by the ladies Maria and Katharine on Lords Longaville and Dumain. For Biron, the condition is more peculiar: he must, over the same twelve-month period, visit the sick and dying, and attempt to make them smile.

The subject of *Love's Labour's Lost* is the disconnect between the way men talk about their conduct in love and the way they do, in fact, conduct themselves. The oath to abstain from contact with women is almost broken before it is given, the humour arising from the fact that while each and every man breaks the oath, each and every man also expects the others to uphold it: we accordingly have the absurd spectacle of the King exposing his default before Biron, Longaville exposing his default before Biron and the King, and Dumain exposing his default before the three of them, in each case the observers feeling entitled to criticize the others for exactly the default which they themselves have committed. It is through this device that Shakespeare communicates a broader point: that hypocrisy in matters of the heart is endemic and found in men across the board, not least in those who profess themselves above all that.

When these men do proceed, in defiance of their oaths, to make contact with and woo the ladies, they do so in a way that expresses self-love every bit as much as it does love for an independent other. In a formulaic manner, each of them pens a verse in praise of his preferred lady before he has even made an effort to exchange words with her: their attention is on themselves, rather than the supposed objects of their affections. This is what the ladies successfully expose when they disguise themselves as each other: none of the men recognizes that he is wooing the wrong lady, because none of them really knows the lady he was intending to woo in the first place.

What makes *Love's Labour's Lost* memorable and distinctive is the twist whereby death intervenes where there would (in a more typical comedy) normally be marriage: as Shakespeare puts it, 'Our wooing doth not end like an old play: Jack hath not Jill.' The fact of death changes the mood immediately; it gives the work an unexpected depth. In this context, the shallowness of the men's affections becomes painfully obvious: they continue to pursue their amorous intentions in the face of a personal tragedy for the Princess, when true lovers would know immediately that courtship must take second place. The men are not bad; they are simply not yet ready. What they need—as Rosaline intuits—is to focus their wit on pleasing others rather than on pleasing themselves: this is why she demands that Biron attend on the sick and the dying. In the final analysis, then, *Love's Labour's Lost* points us in the direction of personal growth—towards seeking a fuller understanding of the needs of others, even in circumstances where that is the last thing on our minds.

LOVE'S LABOUR'S LOST

It was the pleasant whim of the King of Navarre and his friends, the Lords Biron, Longaville, and Dumain, to vow one day that they would devote themselves to study for three years and see no woman during all that time. Their court, said the King, should be a little Academe, and Navarre the wonder of the world, for they would war against their affections and desires and live a contemplative life.

When the time came for subscribing their names to this agreement, Longaville and Dumain were ready to do it without delay; but Biron held out, being of a gallant nature and loving the company of ladies, as secretly did all the rest, and was for argument and amendment of the plan. He was willing, he said, to live secluded and study for three years; but there were other strict observances, such as not to see a woman during that term; not to touch food on one day in each week; to take but one meal every day, and to sleep only three hours in the night, yet not be seen to wink through the morning. These things he said he wished might not be enrolled in the bond, for they were barren tasks and too hard to keep.

The King made answer that Biron's oath was already passed, but the reluctant lord replied that he had sworn to no conditions, saving only to study and stay three years in the court.

Then the others in chorus vowed that he had sworn to all the conditions, but he held that it was only in jest. 'What, after all, is the end of study?' asked Biron. 'To know that which else you should not know,' answered the King.

At this the gay Lord Biron turned the subject, which was growing serious, with a jest, and said he would study, then, the things he was forbidden to know, as where he might dine well when he was expressly bidden to fast; or where to meet some lady when he was denied her company; or, having sworn to a crabbed oath, study how to break it. 'Swear me to this,' quoth he, 'and I will never say no.'

He would not listen to the chiding of the King, but railed on pleasantly, like the merry-hearted gentleman he was. 'Study,' he said, 'is like the heaven's glorious sun, that will not be searched by saucy glances; and, moreover, continual plodders have won little enough from their books saving base authority. The earthly godfathers that give the names to the stars have no more profit from their shining than common folk that do not know what they are. To know too much is to get nothing but fame, which is cheap enough, since every godfather can give it.'

Hereupon the three others began to rally Biron for his show of the very knowledge he mocked at; but he held his own in the passage of wit, and at last the King was forced to cry, 'Well, go home, then, Biron, if you will. Adieu!' and was for bowing him out of the compact. But here the true-heartedness of Biron showed itself through his gaiety, for he said, 'No, my good lord; I have sworn to stay with you, and, though I have spoken more for barbarism than you can say for the angel knowledge, yet I'll keep my oath and bide the penance.' He took the paper and began to read it aloud:

'Item, That no woman shall come within a mile of my court, on pain of losing her tongue.

'Item, If any man be seen to walk with a woman within the term of three years he shall endure such public shame as the rest of the court shall possibly devise.'

Here, looking up, Biron said to the King, 'My liege, you must break this article yourself, for well you know that the French King's daughter comes here in embassy to speak with you about the surrender of Aquitaine to her bed-ridden father.

Biron now enjoyed a merry triumph, for the King was in dismay. The visit of the Princess had been forgotten, but her mission was of too much importance to be put aside. The King was for dispensing with his decree and entertaining her within his court on the plea of necessity; but Biron took advantage of his weakness, quickly signed the bond, and proclaimed, mockingly, that if he were ever forsworn it would be purely from necessity.

While all this was happening the Princess approached the court of Navarre and sent forward her courtier, Boyet, to tell the King of her arrival. She had in her train, besides this gallant gentleman, the ladies Rosaline, Maria, and Katharine—all light of heart and nimble of wit—and with these and the other lords of her household she gossiped of the King of Navarre and his friends until Boyet's return. He came back presently with the information that the King had received notice of her approach and was well addressed to meet her, but that he meant to lodge her in the fields rather than seek a dispensation of his oath.

As Boyet was telling this to his mistress, the King drew near and welcomed her warmly to his court of Navarre. She haughtily gave him back his fair words, and, as for welcome, she said she had yet found none, for the roof of the court of open air under which they stood was too high to be his, and welcome to the wide fields too base to be hers. This twinged the King shrewdly, and he hastened to offer her welcome to his proper court; upon which she asked him to conduct her thither. Then he told her of his oath, which she pretended to be ignorant of, and she fell to rallying him and was much vexed, asking that he suddenly give his decision in her suit and let her go.

While the King was reading the paper which the Princess now gave him, his friends mingled with the ladies, and each found his match in wit; but when Navarre had finished the paper, he hushed their banter by some grave words to the Princess. 'Madam,' he said, 'your father here intimates the payment of a hundred thousand crowns, which is but the one-half of an entire sum disbursed by my father in his wars. But say that we have received that amount, though we have not, there yet remains unpaid another hundred thousand, in surety of which one part of Aquitaine is bound to us, although it is not valued at the money's worth. If, then, your father, the King, will restore a half of what is unsatisfied, we will give up our right in Aquitaine, and hold fair friendship with him. But it seems he does not purpose even this, for here he demands to have a hundred thousand pounds repaid, and to leave Aquitaine in our possession, which we had much rather give up and have back the money lent by our father.'

Following this, the King said some courtly words to the Princess; but she resented his words about her father and insisted that the sum he demanded had been paid. This Navarre professed never to have heard of, but he said if she could prove it he would pay it back or yield up Aquitaine.

The Princess quickly took him at his word and appealed to Boyet to produce acquittances from the King's father for such a sum. Boyet told her that the package wherein that and other specialties were bound had not come, but that tomorrow she should have a sight of it. Hereupon the King said he would wait, and in the meantime offered such welcome as he could, without breach of honour, tender to her. 'You may not come within my gates, fair princess,' said he, 'but here without you shall be so received as you shall deem yourself lodged in my heart.' Then the King and his attendants bade the ladies farewell and parted for the court, but not without a passage of wit between the ladies attendant on the Princess and the gay courtiers of Navarre.

Now, there was one other who had taken the King's oath of a three years' studious life. He had been chosen because of his droll and fantastic humours. He was described by the King as a refined traveller from Spain, a man planted in the world's newest fashion, who had a mint of phrases in his brain. He was, in truth, one who was ravished by the music of his own vain tongue. This was Don Adriano de Armado, and he was welcomed into the fellowship of study because, as the King said, he might relate the worth of many a knight from tawny Spain, and thus he with Costard the swain could make them sport when they desired it in their solitude.

It happened that Armado had by the King's command placed Costard in durance because of his unlawful conduct with Jaquenetta, a country wench. But Don Armado, in his turn, had also become enamoured of Jaquenetta and he determined to employ Costard to bear a letter to her. For this service he gave the swain his liberty and sent him on his way.

Before very long Costard was met by Lord Biron, who also employed him to deliver a sealed-up letter, which he explained was for Rosaline, who might be overtaken when she came to the park to hunt on that afternoon. Costard took his guerdon and went onward, but Biron lingered under the trees and reproached himself—he that had been love's whip, a very beadle to a humorous sigh, a critic; nay, a night-watch constable; a domineering pedant over Cupid—he to be in love! 'What,' quoth he, 'I love! I sue! I seek a wife! A woman like a German clock, still repairing, ever out of frame, and never going aright! Nay, but to be perjured is worst of all, and among three to love the worst of all!' Then he fell to reviling his lady-love in playful bitterness, but he was past cure, for Cupid had, in very truth, in return for his neglect, imposed a plague which there was no escaping.

At the time appointed by the King, who desired

to entertain his guests as best he could while still remaining true to his oath, the Princess and her retinue were led abroad by one of the royal foresters to a hunt in the park; and, as Biron had directed, Costard followed the train and attempted to deliver Biron's letter to the Lady Rosaline. He asked the Princess, with a loutish bow, which was the head lady; and, as she said she was, he announced that he had a letter from one Monsieur Biron to one Lady Rosaline. Hereupon the Princess demanded the letter, and it was handed to Boyet, who, looking at the superscription, said, 'This letter is mistook. It importeth none here. It is writ to Jaquenetta;' for the silly swain had delivered Don Armado's letter instead of Lord Biron's. The Princess commanded that the wax be broken; and the Spanish don's letter, full of hard words and bombastic phrases, was read amid peals of laughter.

Then the Princess called Costard: 'Thou fellow, a word: Who gave thee this letter?' The swain answered that my lord had given it to him, and that it was from my lord to my lady. 'From which lord to which lady?' said the Princess. 'From my Lord Biron, a good master of mine, to a lady of France that he called Rosaline.' 'Thou hast mistaken his letter,' said the Princess, and she and her train rode gaily away.

Strolling through the park after them came Jaquenetta and Costard, who were overtaken by two men very learned in their own conceit—namely, Holofernes, a schoolmaster, and Sir Nathaniel, a curate, with whom was Dull, the constable. Jaquenetta interrupted the pompous discourse of these two and asked the parson to be so good as to read her a letter which she held forth to him. It was given her by Costard, she said, and was sent her from Don Armatho, as she miscalled her Spanish suitor.

Sir Nathaniel, urged by Holofernes, began to, read the letter aloud, which was really that of Lord Biron to Rosaline. It was in verse, and breathed a great love to that lady, calling her by many endearing names. 'But, damosella virgin,' asked Holofernes, in his high-flown speech, 'was this directed to you?' Jaquenetta answered that it was; but upon looking at the superscription, Holofernes found the true address: 'To the snow-white hand of the most beauteous Lady Rosaline,' and, turning to Jaquenetta, he bade her go deliver it into the hands of the King, for, seeing that Lord Biron had entered into compact with the King for three years' withdrawal from womankind, it might concern him much. Taking Costard with her, Jaquenetta thereupon hurried away, and the two pedants strolled on in fantastical converse.

After all these were gone, Biron came through the trees with a paper in his hand, much berating himself for having, in self-despite, fallen madly in love. 'By the world,' he muttered, 'I would not care a pin if the other three were in,' for this was his only hope of escape from his hard bargain. But at that moment he saw one of his vow-fellows coming forward, also with a paper in his hand. To conceal his own embarrassment, and secretly to learn, at the same time, what had happened to the King, for it was he who approached, Biron climbed into a tree and screened himself among its thick leaves. 'Ah, me!' sighed the melancholy King, and Lord Biron, in his high perch whispered to himself, with inward satisfaction, 'Shot, by Heaven!'

The King then began to read aloud a set of verses made to a lady whose beauty he placed above the sun and moon; but, alas! she would still make him weep. He was about to drop the paper, addressed to the Princess, in the hope that she would find it, when he heard a footstep on the grass near to him, and stepped aside with his poem still in his hand.

Just as the King disappeared in the deep shade of the trees, Longaville came through the trunks, reading aloud to himself. Biron above, among the leaves, mocked at them both under his breath and was mightily pleased to find his forlorn hope thus coming true. As Longaville reproached himself for his faithlessness to his fellows, Biron and the King, unknown to each other, interjected their comment between his words, each after his own mood, for the King was sad at the miscarriage of his plan, but Biron, as usual, appeared to take it in a merry spirit.

Longaville now read his verses aloud, which assured the fair lady that in addressing her he did not break his vow to forswear women, as she was a goddess. His vow was earthly, but she was a heavenly love. 'What fool,' he said, 'is not wise enough to lose an oath in order to win a paradise?'

As Longaville finished this plausible piece of logic, and was wondering how he should send the missive to the lady it celebrated, forward came Dumain, also with a paper in his hand and also in the musing mien of a lover. Longaville stepped hastily aside when he saw his fellow courtier, and he also in turn became an eavesdropper. Biron from his perch laughed in his sleeve at them and thought how like it was to the old infant play of 'All hid,' while he sat in the sky like a demigod, knowing the secrets of all the wretched fools below him.

Dumain exclaimed, with a great sigh, 'O most divine Kate!' and Biron in his glee answered, aside, 'O most profound coxcomb!' Dumain continued to call his chosen lady by all sorts of fair names, as is the wont of lovers, and Biron mocked each sentence with some outlandish simile; but the others put in now and then a word of sympathy. At last Dumain began to read the ode he had been intent upon, and all were still, for it was one of the sweetest and archest of love-songs:

'On a day (alack the day!),
Love, whose month is ever May,
Spied a blossom, passing fair,
Playing in the wanton air.
Through the velvet leaves the wind,
All unseen, 'gan passage find;
That the lover, sick to death,
Wish'd himself the heaven's breath.
Air, quoth he, thy cheeks may blow;
Air, would I might triumph so!
But, alack! my hand is sworn
Ne'er to pluck thee from thy thorn.
Vow, alack! for youth unmeet;
Youth so apt to pluck a sweet.
Do not call it sin in me,
That I am forsworn for thee:
Thee for whom Jove would swear
Juno but an Ethiope were;
And deny himself for Jove,
Turning mortal for thy love.'

He ended with another sigh made up of satisfaction with his ode, of his hopeless suing, and of his pang for a broken vow; then said he, 'I will send this and something else more plain that shall express my true love's ardour. O, would,' he exclaimed, 'the King, Biron, and Longaville were lovers too!'

Longaville could stand the suspense no longer. He advanced from the shadow of the trees and roundly chided his friend. 'Dumain,' he said, 'your love is uncharitable that wants society in its grief. You may look pale, but I should blush to be overheard and taken napping so.'

At this the King stepped out and confronted Longaville, who was as much astonished to have been discovered as Dumain. 'Come, sir,' said the King to Longaville, 'Blush yourself; your case is the same as his, and in chiding him you offend twice.' Then he went mercilessly over the words of Longaville's sonnet to Maria, and told at last how he had been closely shrouded in the bushes and had marked the actions of both and blushed for them. 'What will Biron say,' he continued, 'when he hears of these broken pledges? Think how he will scorn you and spend his wit upon you! How he will triumph, and leap, and laugh at it! I would not have him know so much of me for all the wealth I ever saw!'

Biron now thought it was time to show himself. He descended from the tree where he had been in hiding, and straightway began to reproach the King. 'Ah, good my liege, I pray pardon me,' said he, with a dutiful bow; 'but, good heart, what grace have you thus to reprove these worms for loving, who are yourself more in love than they?' Then Biron, in turn, repeated all the conceits of the King's love ditty, who was in dismay thus to be found out in the presence of those he had just condemned for committing his very fault.

Biron, knowing the state of his own heart, rejoiced at the opportunity to cover his default by reproving it in the others. He rallied them and gave them good advice by turns. 'O, what a scene of foolery,' he cried, 'of sighs, groans, sorrow, and tears! Where does your grief lie, tell me, good Dumain? Where is your pain, gentle Longaville; and where is my liege's? All about the breast—A caudle, ho!'

'Your fun is too bitter,' said the indignant King; but Biron ran on with laughter and mockery, asking at last, 'When did you ever know me to write a thing in rhyme? When did you ever hear me praise a hand, a foot, a face, or an eye?' Yet like all who carry a jest beyond bounds, for none of us are without our faults, Biron's banter at last brought him to shame. He was about to run away, still shaking his sides with laughter, when someone approached and he stopped an instant to learn who it was.

'God bless the King!' said Jaquenetta, for it was she and Costard, who had come to seek His Majesty with Biron's verses, as Holofernes had recommended. Jaquenetta begged that the letter which she handed to the King should be in his presence read, for the parson misdoubted that it was treason. The King gave the paper to Biron and asked him to read it, meanwhile questioning where it had come from. Costard said he had had it from Don Armado, upon which the King noticed that Biron was destroying it. 'How now! What are you doing? Why do you tear it?' he asked abruptly. 'A toy, my liege, a toy; Your Grace need not be alarmed,' was Biron's evasive reply; but it stood him in little stead, for Longaville had noticed how the paper moved him to passion, and Dumain picked up one of the pieces with Biron's name written upon it. Then Biron fell to cursing Costard, who had been born, he said, to do him shame; and, fairly beaten, he cried, 'Guilty, my lord, guilty; I confess, I confess!' 'What?' asked the King. 'That you three fools lacked me to make up the sum. We are all pickpurses in love, my liege, and deserve to die.'

Costard hereupon, with scorn for all traitors, passed on with Jaquenetta and left the nobles to their mutual explanations.

Biron and the King vied with one another in praise of their ladyloves until finally all fell to jeering at the choice of Biron, who defended his Rosaline like the gallant lover and wit he was. When they had pleasantly bantered each other thus for a long time, the King and the rest called upon Biron, in recognition of his nimble mind, to prove their loving to be lawful and their faith unbroken. This, in some noble words which showed him to be as deep in thought as he was light in converse, Biron quickly did after a manner which all approved. Then the four lovers ran off to prepare some sport for their mistresses, Biron gaily singing a song as they passed away under the trees.

In the meantime, the ladies had assembled in the park, near the pavilion of the Princess, and had read the verses sent them by their ardent wooers. As they stood under the shade, laughing lightly over these, Boyet approached in his gayest mood and asked eagerly for the Princess. When she appeared he told her how he had lain down for rest half an hour under the cool shade of a sycamore, and there had overheard the King and his companions plotting to come thither disguised as Russians and make trial of the affections of their chosen mistresses. They had also planned to send forward in advance a pretty knavish page, whom they had well taught what he was to say.

The ladies soon resolved that they would have a counter-device with which to meet the gallants. They straightway masked and changed favours, so that the King and his courtiers must each choose the wrong partner. They had hardly done this before the King's page came forward through the wood and hailed them as 'the richest beauties on the earth.' This the ladies resented by turning their backs; but the page, who was quick in answers, made a happy retort, while Biron and the rest, who were behind him, urged him on to repeat the words they had taught him. Rosaline, disguised as the Princess, and feigning not to know who these strangers were, asked Boyet to learn what they sought. They replied that they wanted nothing but peace and gentle visitation, upon which Rosaline bade them to be gone. The King told her, supposing her to be her royal mistress, that they had measured many miles for the favour of a dance on the grass with her and her companions; but she would and she would not, and finally they separated into pairs, the King going aside with Rosaline, Biron with the Princess, Dumain with Maria, and Longaville with Katharine, each supposing he had found his own choice, and each meeting with a merry defiance, which finally drove them all away.

The ladies fell then to telling what the gallants had said, and the mirth ran high as their mistaken confessions of love were repeated. At last the Princess asked what they should do if the lovers returned in their own shapes. Rosaline was for mocking them still by telling them how a band of fools had come there disguised like Russians, and that the Princess and her ladies wondered what they were and to what end they had brought thither their shallow shows and vilely-penned prologue. Just as they had resolved on this course the gallants reappeared in their proper habits, and the ladies whipped into their tents to prepare to receive them anew.

When the Princess and her attendants, led by Boyet, came forth to greet her royal guest, the King made her a fair all hail, but she returned a light answer. He told her that he and his companions had come to lead her company to his court; but she appeared to resent his former discourtesy and refused to go with him. He took shame to himself for the coldness of her welcome, and said that he was distressed that she had lived thus in desolation, unseen and unvisited. 'Not so, my lord,' said the Princess. 'We have had pastimes and pleasant games. A mess of Russians left us but now.' 'How, madam? Russians?' said the King. 'Yes, in truth, my lord. Trim gallants, full of state and courtship.' Hereupon Rosaline spoke up. 'It is not so, my lord,' said she. 'We four were indeed confronted by four men in Russian habit, who stayed here an hour, and talked apace, but in the whole hour they did not bless us with a single happy word. I dare not call them fools; but I will say that, when they are thirsty, fools would fain have a drink.'

Thus rallying Navarre and his courtiers, the ladies brought them at last to a confession of their trick; but even then the gallants were ignorant of the deception that had previously been played upon them. When the King vowed that he had whispered a pledge of love into his lady's ear, the Princess charged that if she should challenge him with this he would reject her. 'Upon my honour, no!' said he, warmly. 'Forbear,' cried the Princess. 'You have broken your oath once!' 'Despise me, then,' said he, 'when I break this oath.' 'I will: therefore you must keep it. Rosaline, what did the Russian whisper in your ear?'

Rosaline repeated the King's oath made to her when in disguise as the Princess, and the Princess feigned to take the King at his word and joyfully gave

115

him Rosaline's hand. Navarre was vexed and put out of countenance by this, and only after a free explanation of the pleasant device of the ladies could he and his companions understand how they had been caught in a trap laid by themselves.

But Costard came in at this moment to announce a mummery which he and his companions had planned for the entertainment of the Princess, and the embarrassment of the gallants was soon lost in the fun of the play. When this mock drama was about to end in a real combat between Costard and Armado, arrived a messenger from France to the Princess, named Mercade, who brought tidings of her old father's death. Upon this news the company quickly dispersed, and the Princess, in her sudden sorrow, gave orders for her departure on that same night. She thanked the King and his companions for all their fair endeavours, and entreated them to excuse the liberties she and her companions had appeared to take. If they had borne themselves over-boldly, the King's gentleness was guilty of it. 'Farewell, worthy lord!' said she. 'A heavy heart does not bear a humble tongue. Excuse me for coming so short of thanks for my great suit so easily obtained.'

But the King would not be put off. He was truly in love with the Princess, and even her great grief could not prevent him from urging his suit. 'Since love's argument was on foot first,' said he, 'do not let sorrow jostle it from its purpose. To wail for lost friends is not so wholesome as to rejoice at friends newly found.'

The Princess still feigned to misunderstand his declaration of love, so he spoke in honest, plain words which should best pierce the ears of grief. He told the ladies how, for their sakes, he and his gentlemen had neglected time, and played foul with their oaths. How beauty had deformed them, drawn them aside from their intents, and made them appear ridiculous, for love is wanton as a child, skipping, and vain, and formed by the eye, like which, it is full of stray shapes varying in subjects as the eye rolls to every varied object.

The Princess replied that they had received the letters of the King and his companions, with all their favours and messages of love; but had rated them as pleasant jests to while away the time, not as serious professions.

The King then made one last appeal that their vows might be accepted in very truth, but still the Princess held out. The time was too short, she said, to make a world-without-end bargain in. Yet there was one condition on which she might at length accept his wooing. Still rallying him for his foolish pledge of retirement which he had so quickly broken, she said she would not accept his oath; but if he would go with speed to some forlorn and naked hermitage remote from the pleasures of the world, and stay there a year, then, if that austere and unsociable life should not change the state of his heart and make him regret an offer made in heat of blood, he might come and claim her hand, by the virgin palm of which, now held against his, she swore to be his wife. Until then she would shut herself up in a house of mourning and shed endless tears for the death of the old king, her father.

When Navarre had dutifully accepted these hard conditions, and said some ardent words of adieu, Biron, Dumain, and Longaville asked each in turn of his chosen lady what was to be his fate, and each had for answer that he must come a-wooing at the end of a twelvemonth and a day, when the King came to the Princess. Then Biron, in the excess of his ardour, asked Rosaline to impose some service on him that might fitly show his love.

'I have often heard of you, my Lord Biron,' returned Rosaline, who had a store of light wit, but who had withal much womanly wisdom and loved seriousness none the less. 'The world's large tongue proclaims you to be a man full of mockeries and wounding jests. If, then, you would win me, and at the same time weed this wormwood from your brain, you must, for a twelvemonth to come, visit the sick from day to day and converse with groaning wretches, your task being to force them to smile at your witty sallies.' 'But what jest could move laughter in the throat of death?' asked Biron, in dismay. 'It is impossible. Mirth cannot move a soul that is in agony.' He was beginning thus to realize how small a part of life lies in laughter, which to him had hitherto been the all in all.

'Why,' said Rosaline, not a little pleased to find him

so easily schooled, 'that is the way to choke a gibing spirit whose influence is begotten of the grace that shallow hearers give to fools. A jest's prosperity lies in the ear of the hearer, never in the tongue of the maker. So, if ears that are deaf with the noise of their own groans will listen to your idle mockeries, continue them, and I will have you and the fault together. But if they will not, throw away that spirit, and I will be right joyful at your reformation.'

Biron was too deep in love to resist any condition that Rosaline might impose upon him. He gladly accepted her terms, and said he would, whatever befell, jest for the year long in a hospital.

Then the Princess turned to depart, but the King

offered to take her on her way, while Biron, jester to the last, remarked that their wooing had not ended like an old play. 'Jack has not got Jill,' quoth he. 'The courtesy of these ladies might well have made our sport a comedy.' 'Come, sir,' said the King, 'it wants but a twelvemonth and it will end.' 'But that's too long for a play,' ruefully said Biron.

Here broke in Don Armado, desiring to kiss the royal finger and crying that he had vowed to Jaquenetta to hold the plough three years for her sweet love. 'But, most esteemed greatness,' pleaded he, 'will you hear the dialogue that the two learned men, Holofernes and Sir Nathaniel, have made in praise of the owl and the cuckoo?' The King bade him call them forth quickly, and out stepped the two pedants with Moth and Costard, whereupon Ver, the Spring, sang a song of the cuckoo, and Hiems, or Winter, this ditty of the owl:

'When icicles hang by the wall,
And Dick the shepherd blows his nail,
And Tom bears logs into the hall,
And milk comes frozen home in pail,
When blood is nipp'd, and ways be foul,
Then nightly sings the staring owl,
To-who;
To-whit, to-who, a merry note,
While greasy Joan doth keel the pot.

'When all aloud the wind doth blow,

And coughing drowns the parson's saw,
And birds sit brooding in the snow,
And Marian's nose looks red and raw;
When roasted crabs hiss in the bowl,
Then nightly sings the staring owl,
To-who;
To-whit, to-who, a merry note,
While greasy Joan doth keel the pot.'

5

A MIDSUMMER NIGHT'S DREAM

INTRODUCTION

Imperious nobles and star-crossed lovers, a mysterious woodland on a hot summer's night, a fairy king and fairy queen at odds over possession of a changeling boy, a mischief-making sprite, and a magical resolution that heals all wrongs and brings men and women together in nuptial celebration—this one has it all and more. Of all Shakespeare's tales, none is more enchanting and none more delightful than A *Midsummer Night's Dream*.

The setting is Athens where the Duke Theseus and his Amazonian bride, Hippolyta, are preparing to wed. Meanwhile, a young lady of Athens, Hermia, has been commanded, on pain of death, to marry Demetrius—when in fact she loves another young

Athenian, Lysander. In defiance, Hermia decides to elope with Lysander, and arranges to meet him that midsummer night in a wood outside the city. Unfortunately for her, she makes the mistake of telling her friend Helena about the plan. Helena recounts the news to Demetrius, whom she loves, and Demetrius heads to the wood in pursuit, himself being followed by Helena. Fortuitously, the fairy king Oberon and his fairy queen Titania are to meet in the wood on that same night. They too are at odds: Oberon requires to have given to him a changeling boy, but Titania has refused to surrender the boy because his mother had been her friend. To punish Titania's disobedience, Oberon instructs a mischievous sprite by the name of 'Puck' to obtain magical juice derived from a flower called 'love-in-idleness', which when applied to the eyes of a sleeping person will make them fall in love with the first thing they see. Puck applies the juice to the eyes of Titania who, on waking, falls immediately in love with a man whose head Oberon has, by magic, turned into that of an ass. Puck is also, on instructions from Oberon, directed to apply the juice to the eyes of Demetrius in order that he will fall in love with Helena, but Puck mistakenly applies it to the eyes of Lysander instead: this results in Lysander falling in love with Helena, who is in love with Demetrius, who is in love with Hermia, who is in love with Lysander. Oberon directs Puck to reapply the juice again so that the Athenians will be correctly paired off, and, having obtained the changeling boy from Titania, also corrects her eyesight too. The two pairs of Athenian lovers prepare for their respective nuptials, Theseus and Hippolyta are ready to wed, and the rift between fairy king and fairy queen is healed.

The tale of A *Midsummer Night's Dream* has a deep quasi-mystical message about stability, the birth of disorder, and the restoration of order. The stable social order of the tale hinges upon a series of paired and harmonious opposites constituted by masculine and feminine polarities: in the human world, these polarities are represented by Theseus, ruler of Athens, and his bride Hippolyta, queen of the Amazons; and in the supernatural world, by the fairy king Oberon and his fairy queen Titania. Disorder arises when one polarity (the masculine) becomes excessively dominant or where the other polarity (the feminine) becomes excessively resistant. In the human world, disruption occurs when Egeus demands his daughter marry a man she does not love, invoking the Athenian law providing that she be put to death if she refuse. At the same time, in the supernatural world, disruption arises as a result of Oberon's requiring Titania to surrender a fairy boy to him. Order is restored when the polarities re-align harmoniously once again: each of the human lovers is paired, the fairy king and queen reconciled, and the social orders brought together in a night of shared festivity and joy.

The return to order is brought about to a

considerable degree by the activities of a character called 'Puck'. 'Pouk' was, in fact, a medieval term for the devil, depicted as a frightening, rough, and hairy creature, who was also a malevolent shapeshifter. Shakespeare re-envisages the figure as a mischief-maker—Puck's preferred activities being comical pranks in neighbouring villages, such as getting into the dairies and skimming the milk, dancing in butter-churn, spoiling the ale, and pulling away the stools of old ladies to make them fall over when they try to sit down. At the same time, it is Puck who is entrusted with playing precisely the tricks that bring order back into a disordered world. Shakespeare's message is profound: when order has failed, it is unlikely to be capable of re-asserting itself, especially where it was the excess of order that caused the problem in the first place; in these circumstances, it is, paradoxically, the agents of mischief and disorder that are best placed to restore balance.

In the final analysis, the vision Shakespeare presents is of a world in harmonious but delicate equipoise between the forces of order and disorder, masculine and feminine, and dark and light, as well as between the respective social classes of rulers, citizens, and labourers. There isn't the slightest suggestion that Shakespeare would approve of the inversion of these polarities, the erosion of differences, or the confusion of categories. Shakespeare does, on the other hand, show a deep appreciation of the risks of enforcing the status quo in too dogmatic or unyielding a manner. It is by maintaining the natural balance of things in a tolerant and flexible way, and by accepting the role to be played by forces of mischief and disorder, that communities can survive and prosper.

A MIDSUMMER NIGHT'S DREAM

There was a law in the city of Athens which gave to its citizens the power of compelling their daughters to marry whomsoever they pleased; for upon a daughter's refusing to marry the man her father had chosen to be her husband, the father was empowered by this law to cause her to be put to death; but as fathers do not often desire the death of their own daughters, even though they do happen to prove a little refractory, this law was seldom or never put in execution, though perhaps the young ladies of that city were not unfrequently threatened by their parents with the terrors of it.

There was one instance, however, of an old man, whose name was Egeus, who actually did come before Theseus (at that time the reigning Duke of Athens), to complain that his daughter Hermia, whom he had commanded to marry Demetrius, a young man of a noble Athenian family, refused to obey him, because she loved another young Athenian, named Lysander. Egeus demanded justice of Theseus, and desired that this cruel law might be put in force against his daughter.

Hermia pleaded in excuse for her disobedience, that Demetrius had formerly professed love for her dear friend Helena, and that Helena loved Demetrius to distraction; but this honourable reason, which Hermia gave for not obeying her father's command, moved not the stern Egeus.

Theseus, though a great and merciful prince, had no power to alter the laws of his country: therefore he could only give Hermia four days to consider of it; and at the end of that time, if she still refused to marry Demetrius, she was to be put to death.

When Hermia was dismissed from the presence of the Duke, she went to her lover Lysander, and told him the peril she was in, and that she must either give him up and marry Demetrius, or lose her life in four days.

Lysander was in great affliction at hearing these evil tidings; but recollecting that he had an aunt who lived at some distance from Athens, and that at the place where she lived the cruel law could not be put in force against Hermia (this law not extending beyond the boundaries of the city), he proposed to Hermia that she should steal out of her father's house that night, and go with him to his aunt's house, where he would marry her. 'I will meet you,' said Lysander, 'in the wood a few miles without the city; in that delightful wood where we have so often walked with Helena in the pleasant month of May.'

To this proposal Hermia joyfully agreed; and she told no one of her intended flight but her friend

Helena. Helena (as maidens will do foolish things for love) very ungenerously resolved to go and tell this to Demetrius, though she could hope no benefit from betraying her friend's secret, but the poor pleasure of following her faithless lover to the wood; for she well knew that Demetrius would go thither in pursuit of Hermia.

The wood in which Lysander and Hermia proposed to meet was the favourite haunt of those little beings known by the name of fairies.

Oberon the king, and Titania the queen of the fairies, with all their tiny train of followers, in this wood held their midnight revels.

Between this little king and queen of sprites there happened, at this time, a sad disagreement; they never met by moonlight in the shady walks of this pleasant wood, but they were quarrelling, till all their fairy elves would creep into acorn-cups and hide themselves for fear.

The cause of this unhappy disagreement was Titania's refusing to give Oberon a little changeling boy, whose mother had been Titania's friend; and upon her death the fairy queen stole the child from its nurse, and brought him up in the woods.

The night on which the lovers were to meet in this wood, as Titania was walking with some of her maids of honour, she met Oberon attended by his train of fairy courtiers.

'Ill met by moonlight, proud Titania,' said the fairy king. The queen replied: 'What, jealous Oberon, is it you? Fairies, skip hence; I have foresworn his company.' 'Tarry, rash fairy,' said Oberon. 'Am not I thy lord? Why does Titania cross her Oberon? Give me your little changeling boy to be my page.'

'Set your heart at rest,' answered the queen. 'Your whole fairy kingdom buys not the boy of me.' She then left her lord in great anger. 'Well, go your way,' said Oberon. 'Before the morning dawns I will torment you for this injury.'

Oberon then sent for Puck, his chief favourite and privy counsellor.

Puck (or as he was sometimes called, Robin Goodfellow) was a shrewd and knavish sprite, that used to play comical pranks in the neighbouring villages; sometimes getting into the dairies and skimming the milk, sometimes plunging his light and airy form into the butter-churn, and while he was dancing his fantastic shape in the churn, in vain the dairymaid would labour to change her cream into butter; nor had the village swains any better success: whenever Puck chose to play his freaks in the brewing copper, the ale was sure to be spoiled. When a few good neighbours were met to drink some comfortable ale together, Puck would jump into the bowl of ale in the likeness of a roasted crab, and when some old goody was going to drink he would bob against her lips, and spill the ale over her withered chin; and presently after, when the same old dame was gravely seating herself to tell her neighbours a sad and melancholy story, Puck would slip her threelegged stool from under her, and down toppled the poor old woman, and then the old gossips would hold their sides and laugh at her, and swear they never wasted a merrier hour.

'Come hither, Puck,' said Oberon to this little merry wanderer of the night. 'Fetch me the flower which maids call Love in Idleness; the juice of that little purple flower, laid on the eyelids of those who sleep, will make them, when they awake, dote on the first thing they see. Some of the juice of that flower I will drop on the eyelids of my Titania when she is asleep; and the first thing she looks upon when she opens her eyes she will fall in love with, even though it be a lion or a bear, a meddling monkey, or a busy ape; and before I will take this charm from off her sight, which I can do with another charm I know of, I will make her give me that boy to be my page.'

Puck, who loved mischief to his heart, was highly diverted with this intended frolic of his master, and ran to seek the flower; and while Oberon was waiting the return of Puck, he observed Demetrius and Helena enter the wood: he overheard Demetrius reproaching Helena for following him, and after many unkind words on his part, and gentle expostulations from Helena, reminding him of his former love and professions of true faith to her, he left her (as he said) to the mercy of the wild beasts, and she ran after him as swiftly as she could.

The fairy king, who was always friendly to true lovers, felt great compassion for Helena; and perhaps, as Lysander said they used to walk by moonlight in this pleasant wood, Oberon might have seen Helena in those happy times when she was beloved by Demetrius. However that might be, when Puck returned with the little purple flower, Oberon said to his favourite: 'Take a part of this flower; there has been a sweet Athenian lady here, who is in love with a disdainful youth; if you find him sleeping, drop some of the love-juice in his eyes, but contrive to do it when she is near him, that the first thing he sees when he awakes may be this despised lady. You will know the man by the Athenian garments which he wears.' Puck promised to manage this matter very dexterously; and then Oberon went, unperceived by Titania, to her bower, where she was preparing to go to rest. Her fairy bower was a bank, where grew wild thyme, cowslips, and sweet violets, under a canopy of woodbine, musk roses, and eglantine. There Titania always slept some part of the night, her coverlet the enamelled skin of a snake, which, though a small mantle, was wide enough to wrap a fairy in.

He found Titania giving orders to her fairies how they were to employ themselves while she slept.

'Some of you,' said Her Majesty, 'must kill cankers in the musk-rose buds, and some wage war with the bats for their leathern wings, to make my small elves coats; and some of you keep watch that the clamorous owl, that nightly hoots, come not near me; but first sing me to sleep.' Then they began to sing this song:

'You spotted snakes with double tongue,
Thorny hedgehogs, be not seen;
Newts and blind-worms do no wrong,
Come not near our Fairy Queen.
Philomel, with melody,
Sing in our sweet lullaby,
Lulla, lulla, lullaby; lulla, lulla, lullaby;
Never harm, nor spell, nor charm,
Come our lovely lady nigh;
So good night with lullaby.'

When the fairies had sung their queen asleep with

this pretty lullaby, they left her to perform the important services she had enjoined them. Oberon then softly drew near his Titania, and dropped some of the love-juice on her eyelids, saying:

'What thou seest when thou dost wake,
Do it for thy true love take.'

But to return to Hermia, who made her escape out of her father's house that night, to avoid the death she was doomed to for refusing to marry Demetrius. When she entered the wood, she found her dear Lysander waiting for her, to conduct her to his aunt's house; but before they had passed half through the wood, Hermia was so much fatigued, that Lysander, who was very careful of this dear lady, who had proved her affection for him even by hazarding her life for his sake, persuaded her to rest till morning on a bank of soft moss, and lying down himself on the ground at some little distance, they soon fell fast asleep. Here they were found by Puck, who, seeing a handsome young man asleep, and perceiving that his clothes were made in the Athenian fashion, and that a pretty lady was sleeping near him, concluded that this must be the Athenian maid and her disdainful lover whom Oberon had sent him to seek; and he naturally enough conjectured that, as they were alone together, she must be the first thing he would see when he awoke; so, without more ado, he proceeded to pour some of the juice of the little purple flower into his eyes. But it so fell out, that Helena came that way, and, instead of Hermia, was the first object Lysander beheld when he opened his eyes; and strange to relate, so powerful was the love charm, all his love for Hermia vanished away, and Lysander fell in love with Helena.

Had he first seen Hermia when he awoke, the blunder Puck committed would have been of no consequence, for he could not love that faithful lady too well; but for poor Lysander to be forced by a fairy love charm to forget his own true Hermia, and to run after another lady, and leave Hermia asleep quite alone in a wood at midnight, was a sad chance indeed.

Thus this misfortune happened. Helena, as has been before related, endeavoured to keep pace with Demetrius when he ran away so rudely from her; but she could not continue this unequal race long, men being always better runners in a long race than ladies. Helena soon lost sight of Demetrius; and as she was wandering about, dejected and forlorn, she arrived at the place where Lysander was sleeping. 'Ah!' said she, 'this is Lysander lying on the ground: is he dead or asleep?' Then, gently touching him, she said: 'Good sir, if you are alive, awake.' Upon this Lysander opened his eyes, and (the love charm beginning to work) immediately addressed her in terms of extravagant love and admiration; telling her she as much excelled Hermia in beauty as a dove does a raven, and that he would run through fire for her sweet sake; and many more such lover-like speeches.

Helena, knowing Lysander was her friend Hermia's lover, and that he was solemnly engaged to marry her, was in the utmost rage when she heard herself addressed in this manner; for she thought (as well she might) that Lysander was making a jest of her. 'Oh!' said she, 'why was I born to be mocked and scorned by every one? Is it not enough, is it not enough, young man, that I can never get a sweet look or a kind word from Demetrius; but you, sir, must pretend in this disdainful manner to court me? I thought, Lysander, you were a lord of more true gentleness.' Saying these words in great anger, she ran away; and Lysander followed her, quite forgetful of his own Hermia, who was still asleep.

When Hermia awoke, she was in a sad fright at finding herself alone. She wandered about the wood, not knowing what was become of Lysander, or which way to go to seek for him. In the meantime Demetrius, not being able to find Hermia and his rival Lysander, and fatigued with his fruitless search, was observed by Oberon fast asleep. Oberon had learnt by some questions he had asked of Puck that he had applied the love charm to the wrong person's eyes; and now having found the person first intended, he touched the eyelids of the sleeping Demetrius with the love juice, and he instantly awoke; and the first thing he saw being Helena, he, as Lysander had done before, began to address love speeches to her; and just at that moment Lysander, followed by Hermia (for through Puck's unlucky mistake it was now become

Hermia's turn to run after her lover) made his appearance; and then Lysander and Demetrius, both speaking together, made love to Helena, they being each one under the influence of the same potent charm.

The astonished Helena thought that Demetrius, Lysander, and her once dear friend Hermia, were all in a plot together to make a jest of her.

Hermia was as much surprised as Helena; she knew not why Lysander and Demetrius, who both before loved her, were now become the lovers of Helena; and to Hermia the matter seemed to be no jest.

The ladies, who before had always been the dearest of friends, now fell to high words together.

'Unkind Hermia,' said Helena, 'it is you have set Lysander on to vex me with mock praises; and your other lover Demetrius, who used almost to spurn me with his foot, have you not bid him call me goddess, nymph, rare, precious, and celestial? He would not speak thus to me, whom he hates, if you did not set him on to make a jest of me. Unkind Hermia, to join with men in scorning your poor friend. Have you forgot our schoolday friendship? How often, Hermia, have we two, sitting on one cushion, both singing one song, with our needles working the same flower, both on the same sampler wrought; growing up together in fashion of a double cherry, scarcely seeming parted! Hermia, it is not friendly in you, it is not maidenly to join with men in scorning your poor friend.'

'I am amazed at your passionate words,' said

Hermia: 'I scorn you not; it seems you scorn me.' 'Ay, do,' returned Helena, 'persevere, counterfeit serious looks, and make mouths at me when I turn my back; then wink at each other, and hold the sweet jest up. If you had any pity, grace, or manners, you would not use me thus.'

While Helena and Hermia were speaking these angry words to each other, Demetrius and Lysander left them, to fight together in the wood for the love of Helena.

When they found the gentlemen had left them, they departed, and once more wandered weary in the wood in search of their lovers.

As soon as they were gone, the fairy king, who with little Puck had been listening to their quarrels, said to him: 'This is your negligence, Puck; or did you do this wilfully?' 'Believe me, king of shadows,' answered Puck, 'it was a mistake; did not you tell me I should know the man by his Athenian garments? However, I am not sorry this has happened, for I think their jangling makes excellent sport.' 'You heard,' said Oberon, 'that Demetrius and Lysander are gone to seek a convenient place to fight in. I command you to overhang the night with a thick fog, and lead these quarrelsome lovers so astray in the dark, that they shall not be able to find each other. Counterfeit each of their voices to the other, and with bitter taunts provoke them to follow you, while they think it is their rival's tongue they hear. See you do this, till they are so weary they can go no farther; and when you find they are asleep, drop the juice of this other flower into Lysander's eyes, and when he awakes he will forget his new love for Helena, and return to his old passion for Hermia; and then the two fair ladies may each one be happy with the man she loves, and they will think all that has passed a vexatious dream. About this quickly, Puck, and I will go and see what sweet love my Titania has found.'

Titania was still sleeping, and Oberon seeing a clown near her, who had lost his way in the wood, and was likewise asleep: 'This fellow,' said he, 'shall be my Titania's true love'; and clapping an ass's head over the clown's, it seemed to fit him as well as if it had grown upon his own shoulders. Though Oberon fixed the ass's head on very gently, it awakened him, and rising up, unconscious of what Oberon had done to him, he went towards the bower where the fairy queen slept.

'Ah! what angel is that I see?' said Titania, opening her eyes, and the juice of the little purple flower beginning to take effect. 'Are you as wise as you are beautiful?'

'Why, mistress,' said the foolish clown, 'if I have wit enough to find the way out of this wood, I have enough to serve my turn.'

'Out of the wood do not desire to go,' said the enamoured queen. 'I am a spirit of no common rate. I love you. Go with me, and I will give you fairies to attend upon you.'

She then called four of her fairies: their names were Pease-blossom, Cobweb, Moth, and Mustard-seed.

'Attend,' said the queen, 'upon this sweet gentleman; hop in his walks, and gambol in his sight; feed him with grapes and apricots, and steal for him the honeybags from the bees. Come, sit with me,' said she to the clown, 'and let me play with your amiable hairy cheeks, my beautiful ass! and kiss your fair large ears, my gentle joy!'

'Where is Pease-blossom?' said the ass-headed clown, not much regarding the fairy queen's courtship, but very proud of his new attendants.

'Here, sir,' said little Pease-blossom.

'Scratch my head,' said the clown. 'Where is Cobweb?'

'Here, sir,' said Cobweb.

'Good Mr Cobweb,' said the foolish clown, 'kill me the red humble bee on the top of that thistle yonder; and, good Mr Cobweb, bring me the honey-bag. Do not fret yourself too much in the action, Mr Cobweb, and take care the honey-bag break not; I should be sorry to have you overflown with a honey-bag. Where is Mustard-seed?'

'Here, sir,' said Mustard-seed. 'What is your will?' 'Nothing,' said the clown, 'good Mr Mustard-seed, but to help Mr Pease-blossom to scratch; I must go to a barber's, Mr Mustard-seed, for methinks I am marvellous hairy about the face.'

'My sweet love,' said the queen, 'what will you have to eat? I have a venturous fairy shall seek the squirrel's hoard, and fetch you some new nuts.' 'I had rather have a handful of dried pease,' said the clown, who with his ass's head had got an ass's appetite. 'But, I pray, let none of your people disturb me, for I have a mind to sleep.'

'Sleep, then,' said the queen, 'and I will wind you

in my arms. O how I love you! How I dote upon you!'
When the fairy king saw the clown sleeping in the
arms of his queen, he advanced within her sight, and
reproached her with having lavished her favours
upon an ass.

This she could not deny, as the clown was then
sleeping within her arms, with his ass's head crowned
by her with flowers.

When Oberon had teased her for some time, he
again demanded the changeling boy; which she,
ashamed of being discovered by her lord with her new
favourite, did not dare to refuse him.

Oberon, having thus obtained the little boy he had
so long wished for to be his page, took pity on the
disgraceful situation into which, by his merry
contrivance, he had brought his Titania, and threw
some of the juice of the other flower into her eyes; and
the fairy queen immediately recovered her senses,
and wondered at her late dotage, saying how she now
loathed the sight of the strange monster.

Oberon likewise took the ass's head from off the
clown, and left him to finish his nap with his own
fool's head upon his shoulders.

Oberon and his Titania being now perfectly
reconciled, he related to her the history of the lovers,
and their midnight quarrels; and she agreed to go
with him and see the end of their adventures.

The fairy king and queen found the lovers and their
fair ladies at no great distance from each other,
sleeping on a grass-plot; for Puck, to make amends

for his former mistake, had contrived with the utmost diligence to bring them all to the same spot, unknown to each other; and he had carefully removed the charm from off the eyes of Lysander with the antidote the fairy king gave to him.

Hermia first awoke, and finding her lost Lysander asleep so near her, was looking at him and wondering at his strange inconstancy. Lysander presently opening his eyes, and seeing his dear Hermia, recovered his reason which the fairy charm had before clouded, and with his reason, his love for Hermia; and they began to talk over the adventures of the night, doubting if these things had really happened, or if they had both been dreaming the same bewildering dream.

Helena and Demetrius were by this time awake; and a sweet sleep having quieted Helena's disturbed and angry spirits, she listened with delight to the professions of love which Demetrius still made to her, and which, to her surprise as well as pleasure, she began to perceive were sincere.

These fair night-wandering ladies, now no longer rivals, became once more true friends; all the unkind words which had passed were forgiven, and they calmly consulted together what was best to be done in their present situation. It was soon agreed that, as Demetrius had given up his pretensions to Hermia, he should endeavour to prevail upon her father to revoke the cruel sentence of death which had been passed against her. Demetrius was preparing to return to Athens for this friendly purpose, when they were surprised with the sight of Egeus, Hermia's father, who came to the wood in pursuit of his runaway daughter.

When Egeus understood that Demetrius would not now marry his daughter, he no longer opposed her marriage with Lysander, but gave his consent that they should be wedded on the fourth day from that time, being the same day on which Hermia had been condemned to lose her life; and on that same day Helena joyfully agreed to marry her beloved and now faithful Demetrius.

The fairy king and queen, who were invisible spectators of this reconciliation, and now saw the happy ending of the lovers' history, brought about through the good offices of Oberon, received so much pleasure, that these kind spirits resolved to celebrate the approaching nuptials with sports and revels throughout their fairy kingdom.

And now, if any are offended with this story of fairies and their pranks, as judging it incredible and strange, they have only to think that they have been asleep and dreaming, and that all these adventures were visions which they saw in their sleep; and I hope none of my readers will be so unreasonable as to be offended with a pretty harmless Midsummer Night's Dream.

6

THE MERRY
WIVES OF
WINDSOR

INTRODUCTION

The Merry Wives of Windsor is Shakespeare's only comedy set firmly and squarely in England. The main figure of interest is Falstaff, Prince Hal's rambunctious companion from the history plays *Henry IV Part I* and *Part II* and *Henry V.* Legend has it that the play was written in fourteen days and on command of Queen Elizabeth who wished to see Falstaff in love.

The story takes place in Windsor. Sir John Falstaff, a fat old knight, has conceived a passion for one Mrs Page, a married woman still attractive enough to beget an 'elderly passion' in him. The neighbour of Mr and

Mrs Page is another married woman by the name of Mrs Ford. Falstaff's interest in Mrs Ford is rather different: Falstaff is hard-up, Mrs Ford's husband is a man well-to-do, and she has control of his purse-strings. Falstaff, his romantic expectations undimmed by his own disadvantaged state, decides to have love-letters sent to both. The wives, appalled at Falstaff's conduct, share information and arrange to have their revenge on him. Mrs Ford's husband, meanwhile, has been apprised of Falstaff's intentions towards his wife, and, in disguise, approaches Falstaff with a plan to test her loyalty. Three times Falstaff attempts to attend upon a tryst that the wives have purported to arrange, but each time—by the wives' careful foresight and planning—he is frustrated. By the conclusion of the tale, Falstaff has been thoroughly chastised for his foolishness, as has Mr Ford for his jealousy, each having had their comeuppance through 'good sport and fair humour'.

Falstaff himself has been said by Orson Welles to be Shakespeare's greatest creation. He is certainly one of the best-loved. Larger than life and endlessly inventive, Falstaff embodies in a single identity the full range and contradictoriness of human nature. Maurice Morgann, colonial administrator and Shakespeare scholar, in *An Essay on the Dramatic Character of Sir John Falstaff* (1777) put it this way. 'He [Falstaff] is a man at once young and old, enterprising and fat, a dupe and a wit, harmless and wicked, weak in principle and resolute by constitution, cowardly

148

in appearance and brave in reality, a knave without malice, a liar without deceit, and a knight, a gentleman, and a soldier without either dignity, decency, or honour. This is a character which, though it may be decompounded, could not, I believe, have been formed, nor the ingredients of it duly mingled, upon any receipt whatever. It required the hand of Shakespeare himself to give to every particular part a relish of the whole, and of the whole to every particular part.'

The Merry Wives of Windsor reveals Shakespeare as a master humourist. It is now generally accepted that there are three major theories of humour. First, the 'superiority theory': this is where laughter expresses feelings of superiority over others or a former version of ourselves. Here, Falstaff's antics bring pleasure because *we* would never behave like that. Second, the 'relief theory': laughter relieves pent-up nervous energy. Here, laughter at Falstaff's ridiculously inappropriate behaviour serves to relieve any social tension of our own. Third, the 'incongruity theory': we laugh at that which is incongruous—that which violates our mental patterns and expectations. Here, fat old man Falstaff makes us laugh by genuinely believing he can arrange a tryst with two attractive married women.

The Merry Wives of Windsor points to a fundamental human flaw with which we are all, to a greater or lesser degree, afflicted. It has been said that insanity is doing the same thing over and over again and expecting different results. Falstaff repeats the same mistake three times in the tale—each time falling for the merry wives' inducements—and does so despite swearing off it each time that it has gone wrong for him; he only learns his lesson after several unnecessary comeuppances. There is, indeed, nothing more human than the triumph of hope over experience—to a certain extent, we live upon it. And if we share nothing else with Falstaff, we share this.

THE MERRY WIVES OF WINDSOR

In the pleasant town of Windsor lived Master Page and his wife, with their daughter Mistress Anne Page, who was both young and comely. It was plain that Mistress Anne had inherited her good looks from her mother, for Mrs Page was, in spite of her matronhood, still winning enough to beget an elderly passion in Sir John Falstaff. This knight was a freebooter of the town, who lived upon his wits and was followed by a band of cut-purses and knaves who throve on his remnant of respectability. He was fat, and unwieldy of gait, and his face was crimsoned by the potations of sack he was forever draining in Mine Host's taproom of the Garter Inn, in which public-house he dwelt.

But Sir John's happy-go-lucky calling was not prosperous. His fellows were idle, and a great charge upon him, for they cost him ten pounds a week in wages, and his pockets were empty. He decided to turn some of them away; but this was not relished by those who were discharged. They were used to the careless life of dependents, and liked little to have to shift for themselves. Bardolph, a withered serving-man, as his master called him, was engaged by the host of the Garter as a tapster; and Sir John was heartily glad to be rid of him, for his thefts were too open; but Nym and Pistol found no honest employment, nor indeed did they want any, but preferred to take to the road as highwaymen on their own account.

Sir John now determined to make his susceptible heart do service to his empty purse. He had conceived a sudden love for the wife of one Master Ford, who was a neighbour of Master Page, and this new fancy he thought he could make of twofold benefit. Ford was a man well-to-do, and Mistress Ford had, quoth Sir John, the command of her husband's purse. He therefore wrote a gallant letter to her, as a final means of restoring his fortunes. In the wide reach of his affections he had also, as was before said, conceived a passion for the elder Mistress Page, and he now wrote her a love letter as well. He asked Nym and Pistol, as they waited upon him in the taproom of the Garter, each to deliver one of the letters to the lady addressed. This they disdainfully refused to do, both because of assumed honour, and because they knew that Falstaff meant soon to cast them off. Sir John, therefore, gave the letters to his page, Robin, and directed him to carry them to Mistress Ford and Mistress Page.

When Falstaff and Robin had gone out, Pistol began to curse the knight, and Nym swore to be revenged. 'I will incense Ford to deal with poison,' said he. 'I will possess him with yellowness,' meaning jealousy. 'Thou art the Mars of malcontents!' cried Pistol, and he in turn vowed to do the like by Page.

When Mistress Page received her letter she was much puzzled to remember what behaviour on her part had encouraged the amorous knight to think that she might return his sudden affections. As she was reading the letter once again in front of her house, and vowing to be revenged upon him for his impudence, Mistress Ford overtook her and asked her for some counsel, saying that were it not for one trifling respect she could come to much honour.

'Hang the trifle, woman,' said Mistress Page; 'take the honour. What is it? Dispense with trifles: what is it?' 'If I would but consent to be lost for an eternal moment or so I could be knighted,' answered Mistress Ford. Then she showed the letter from Sir John which she had just received, and implored Mistress Page to advise her how to be revenged upon the rascal adventurer. When she saw the letter, Mistress Page was even more angry than before, because it was word for word like her own. 'I warrant he hath a thousand of these letters writ with blank space for different names,' said she, 'and these are of the second edition.'

The honest wives then planned a merry revenge upon the old knight, which should cure him forever of his lying flatteries and clumsy deceits. 'Let us appoint him a meeting,' said they. 'Give him a show of comfort in his suit, and lead him on with a fine-baited delay till he hath pawned his horses to Mine Host of the Garter.' 'Nay,' quoth Mistress Ford, 'I will consent to any act of villany against him that may not sully the chariness of our honesty; but if my husband saw this letter it would give eternal food to his jealousy.'

Thus these good wives, feeling themselves injured in their reputations by the knight's presumption, and being the hearty dames of old England they were, set about a revenge which should show them some sport such as they loved, and at the same time punish the offender.

But as Mistress Page and Mistress Ford were about to go indoors, their husbands, accompanied by Pistol and Nym, came up, in earnest talk, for Pistol in the meantime had assured Mr Ford that Sir John affected his wife, and, though Ford endeavoured to conceal his anxiety at the news, yet it was evident that he was violently suspicious. Page, who had heard the same news about Mistress Page from Nym, was in no wise disturbed, but rather chose to believe in his wife than in so notable a rogue.

Ford had brooded jealously over the possibility of his wife's love for Falstaff, and would not be satisfied until he had put her truth to a test. He went, therefore, to Mine Host of the Garter, and, pretending some merriment, offered him a pottle of burnt sack if he would give him admittance to Falstaff under the false name of Brook. It was, he said, only for a jest; and this quite fell in with Mine Host's mood, who was always eager for sport of any kind.

While Ford was putting on his disguise and preparing to visit Sir John, the knight received a call from Mistress Quickly, an elderly woman who was servant to Dr Caius, the French physician of Windsor. She was a notable gossip and just the person to help Mistress Ford and Mistress Page in their plan of revenge. They had chosen her for her wit, which concealed a store of deceit beneath a show of humble ignorance. She came in to Sir John as he was chiding his surly follower Pistol, and, though she gave warning that her errand was secret, Falstaff, who was not a little guileless for all his bravado and boastfulness, assured her that nobody heard, saving his own people. 'Heaven bless them and make them his servants,' exclaimed Mistress Quickly, and then falteringly delivered her message.

It was from Mistress Ford, who, said the good dame, was much courted by the best nobility of the realm, yet heeded them not, but gave willing ear to Sir John's tender messages. He could come to her, she notified him, between ten and eleven o'clock, when her husband would be absent from home. 'Alas! The sweet woman leads an ill life with him,' exclaimed Mistress Quickly. 'He's a very jealousy man; she leads a very fretful life with him, good heart.' 'Ten and eleven,' mused Sir John, entirely deceived. 'Woman, commend me to her; I will not fail her.' 'Why, you say well,' answered the good dame; 'but I have another message to your worship.' Then she told him how Mistress Page had also sent him her hearty commendations. 'And let me tell you in your ear,' continued she, 'she is as virtuous a civil modest wife as any is in Windsor, yet I never knew a woman so dote upon a man; surely, I think you have charms, la; yes, in truth.'

Thus wheedling and flattering, Mistress Quickly coaxed the knight into the trap laid for him by the good wives, and when he had, in the excess of his delight, given her his purse and sent with her his page Robin to be a messenger between himself and Mistress Page, Dame Quickly retired and left him to his joy at having made so profitable a conquest.

While he was in the midst of his exclamations of delight, Bardolph entered his chamber with the news that one Master Brook was below and would fain speak with him. He then handed Sir John a draught of sack from the visitor. This was a bond of good fellowship which the knight could never resist, so he commanded that Master Brook be called in. 'Such Brooks are welcome to me that overflow with liquor,' said he, and, as Bardolph hastened out to bring the guest, again the old knight fell into a cry of delight at having won Mistress Ford and Mistress Page to accept his suit.

Mr Ford, disguised as Mr Brook, now followed Bardolph into Falstaff's chamber, and when the tapster had retired they fell at once to talk of Mr Brook's business. He had come, he said, about a gentlewoman of the town whose name was Ford. 'I have long loved her,' he frankly confessed (which was probable enough, seeing she was his own wife), 'and, I protest to you, bestowed much upon her. But whatever I have merited, either in my mind or in my means, I have received no recompense except bitter experience.'

Then Mr Brook enlarged on his grievances and frankly avowed his purpose, which was that Sir John should lay an amiable siege to the honesty of Ford's wife. 'Use your art of wooing, win her to consent to you; if any man may, you may as soon as any.' Thus appealing to the vanity of the aged gallant, and giving him money which he urged him to spend freely in the attempt, Ford, in the person of Brook, hoped to test the faith of his wife, for he thought, as a warrant for his wish to undo her, that if he could come to her with any detection in his hand, his desires would have instance and argument to commend them.

Falstaff first carefully secured the money, and next gave Brook his hand in witness of the bargain; lastly, he assured him that he should, if he would, have his wish. Brook was not a little shaken by this promise, and almost betrayed himself at the thought of his own shame, which he was thus bargaining for; but he was a determined man and very jealous, and he persisted in his cruel device.

Falstaff then assured Brook that, by appointment, he would be with Ford's wife between ten and eleven: 'for at that time,' said he, 'the jealous rascally knave, her husband, will be forth. Come you to me tonight; you shall know how I speed.' They then parted, and Ford resolved to overtake Sir John with his wife in his own house, between ten and eleven o'clock that same day.

Now, it happened that a certain Dr Caius and Sir Hugh Evans had challenged each other to a duel which had been caused by their rivalry in wooing Anne Page, of whom each was a lover. That day they had gone forth in the fields beyond Windsor to meet in deadly combat with the sword. Mine Host, with Master Page, Shallow, a country justice, and Slender, another suitor of Anne Page, had heard of this, and had gone out to see the sport, which, as was well foreseen, ended in a mere torrent of words, for Mine Host took care that they kept their limbs whole and hacked nothing but the English tongue.

As all these came back to town they met Master Ford on his way to expose the villany of Falstaff, and were invited by him to his house, where he said he had much good cheer to regale them with, and, for their further entertainment, he would show them a monster.

Shallow and Slender and Mine Host excused themselves from going, as they had other engagements; but the rest were bent upon any madness, and crying, 'Have with you to see the monster,' started gaily off under Ford's guidance.

While all this was taking place, Mrs Ford and Mrs Page had been preparing to receive Falstaff. They had directed the servants to bring into the room where Sir John was to visit Mrs Ford a great basket used for carrying soiled linen out to the laundry in Datchet meadow by the Thames riverside. When this had been done, Mrs Ford charged the men to stand ready hard by in the brewhouse, and, when she suddenly called them, to come forth and, without any pause or staggering, to take the basket on their shoulders, carry it to the laundry, and empty it into the muddy ditch by the river. As the men retired, Falstaff's page, little Robin, appeared with the news that his master was at the back door and requested Mrs Ford's company.

Mrs Page put up a warning finger and asked if the boy had been true to her. 'Ay, I'll be sworn,' said he. 'My master knows not of your being here, and hath threatened to put me into everlasting liberty if I tell you of it.' 'Thou'rt a good boy!' said she, and ran away to hide from Sir John; whereupon Mrs Ford called after her to remember her cue; and then told the page to go say to his master that she was alone.

Falstaff came puffing in anon, protesting his love for Mrs Ford in a medley of words which she feigned well to believe, and vowing he wished that her husband were dead, for he would thus make her his own lady. He heaped a score of clumsy compliments on her beauty, and when she modestly protested he asked, 'What made me love thee? Let that persuade thee there's something extraordinary in thee.'

As he was in the midst of his tender speeches, the page cried from within: 'Mistress Ford, Mistress Ford! Here's Mistress Page at the door, sweating and blowing, and looking wildly, and would needs speak with you presently.' Falstaff was dismayed at this news. He ran and ensconced himself behind the arras which hung against the walls, just as Mrs Page entered the room, crying, 'O Mistress Ford, what have you done? You're shamed, you're overthrown, you're undone forever.' Mistress Page pretended, for the benefit of Sir John in hiding, to be very much agitated, but, to cap the climax, Mrs Page told her that her husband was coming thither with all the officers of Windsor, to search for a gentleman that was now there in his house by his wife's consent. Mrs Ford denied it with what show of gravity she could, and Mrs Page went on to harrow the feelings of the knight by imploring her, if there were one hidden there, to convey him out at all hazards. Then Mrs Ford made pretence of confiding in her friend and openly confessed her fault. She said there was a gentleman concealed in the arras, and she feared not her own shame so much as his peril. 'I had rather than a thousand pound he were out of the house,' cried she, in apparent despair.

'For shame; never stand saying, "you had rather",' replied Mrs Page. 'Your husband's here at hand; bethink you of some conveyance; you cannot hide him in the house. Look, here is a basket; if he be of any reasonable stature he may creep in here; and throw foul linen upon him.'

Falstaff now appeared from behind the hangings in a great fright, and begged them to let him see the basket. As he squeezed his huge bulk in, Mrs Page scornfully cried, 'What! Sir John Falstaff! Are these your letters!' But he did not heed her, pleading only to be taken away.

The two dames and the page then piled in the soiled linen on top of the perspiring knight, and Mistress Ford called to her men to bear him out, giving them careful directions anew where the clothes should be taken.

At this moment Master Ford and his companions arrived at the door. He had been telling them his suspicions on the way, but they treated the tale as a jest. As they entered, the huge basket containing the redoubtable Flemish knight was brought forth. Ford stopped and asked the servants sharply whither they were bearing it, and was told, 'To the laundress, forsooth.' Mrs Ford then spoke up. 'You were best meddle with the buck-washing,' said she, and thus, while Ford went on lamenting over his troubles, the fancied source of them was carried away in the wash-basket under his very eyes.

After all the company had gone into the house,

Ford gave them his keys, bidding them ascend to his chambers and seek out whoever was hidden there. Page pleaded with him to be content, and not to shame his wife; but he persisted, and carried all his visitors up to see Falstaff exposed. In the mean time Mrs Page and Mrs Ford were with suppressed laughter enjoying the joke below, and wondering which pleased them most, the discomfiture of Sir John or of Mr Ford. But Mrs Ford had divined that her husband shrewdly suspicioned Falstaff's presence there, and this not a little alarmed her. Mrs Page said she would lay a plot to try that, and they might thus have still more tricks with the amorous knight. They resolved to send Mistress Quickly to him with apologies for throwing him in the water, and to give him another hope, only to betray him to another punishment. He was to be sent for on the morrow at eight o' clock, that they might feign to make him amends.

Ford and his companions came down disappointed of their prey. Page reproached his neighbour for his false suspicions, saying he would not have a distemper of this kind for the wealth of Windsor Castle, and well he might feel so, for a jealous man breeds himself an endless torment, and does untold harm to his kind. Ford now affected to cast off his gloomy humours, and invited all the company in to the dinner which he had promised them, including Mrs Page and his wife. They went in to share the repast, but nevertheless were resolved to make game of their host when the chance came. Before they drew up to the table, Page asked them to come to his house to breakfast in the morning, and after to go a-birding, for he had a fine hawk for the bush. They were in for any sport, said they, and would right gladly, whereupon they sat about the board and fell to with appetite upon Ford's plentiful viands.

Falstaff was in a great temper the next morning, and called for his sack to have a toast in it, that he should be warmed after his bath in the Thames, for his belly was as cold, said he, as if he had swallowed snowballs for pills. He vowed that if ever he were served such another trick he would have his brains taken out and buttered to give to some dog for a New Year's gift. 'The rogues,' growled he to Bardolph, 'tilted me into the river with as little remorse as they would have drowned a litter of puppies, and you may know by my size that I have a kind of alacrity in sinking. I should have drowned but that the shore was shelvy and shallow—a death that I abhor.'

As he was railing on thus, Mistress Quickly arrived, saying she had come from Mrs Ford. 'I have had ford enough: I was thrown into the ford,' said Falstaff, angrily. The good dame pleaded that it was not her mistress's fault. She was in great grief over it. The men, she said, mistook the direction. Then she gave him her message, which was that Mrs Ford's husband went that day a-birding, and she desired him to come to her between eight and nine. 'I must carry her an answer quickly,' quoth she. 'She'll make amends, I warrant you.'

The knight could not resist such a flattering appeal. His vanity was touched, and he saw, too, in the achievement of his designs a remedy for his empty purse. Hence he said he would go. 'And bid her think what a man is,' he added. 'Let her consider his frailty, and then judge of my merit.'

As Quickly went out, Brook came in with a 'Bless you, sir!' He had come to learn what had passed between Sir John and Mrs Ford, and the knight was not a little chagrined to have to tell him of his ill success—not to speak of the scandalous treatment he had received. But he laid all the blame on Ford's jealousy, and vowed he would be thrown into Aetna, as he had been thrown into Thames, before he would leave her thus. He then revealed to Mr Brook that, as Mr Ford had that morning gone a-birding, he had received another embassy of meeting from Mrs Ford, between eight and nine; and bid Brook come to him at his convenient leisure to know how he sped.

The knight then went out to keep his appointment, and Ford, in the disguise of Brook, was dismayed by the unexpected turn of affairs. He did not quite know whether he was asleep or awake. But he felt that he must overcome his astonishment and act promptly. Falstaff was even then on the way to his house, and he decided to go at once and take him in his villany. As Ford, accompanied by Master Page, Shallow, Dr Caius, and Sir Hugh Evans, came up to the doorway of his house, Mrs Ford, to tease him and to throw him off his guard, had the clothesbasket again carried out, which seeing, Ford raved against his wife and demanded to look into it. In the meanwhile Mrs Page led forth a fat old woman whom she called mother Pratt. This was the aunt of Mrs Ford's maid, and she lived in Brentford. Ford had a great hatred of her and had forbid her his house, and now, in the excess of his anger at not finding Falstaff where he had expected him to be, he beat the old woman unmercifully from his door, calling her witch, and hag, and baggage, and many more unsavory names. Mrs Page reproached him for his cruelty. 'Are you not ashamed?' said she. 'I think you have killed the poor woman.' But Ford only muttered the more curses after her; and when she had hurried her unwieldy body, in ill-fitting clothes with a muffler about her head, out of the way, he prayed his companions to follow him upstairs and discover the hidden rogue.

As they went up, Mrs Ford and Mrs Page gave vent
anew to their glee at this happy device for punishing
the rascally old knight. He had come according to
appointment, and again Mrs Page had brought the
news of Mr Ford's approach. Then Sir John in craven
fear had looked everywhere for a refuge, and had
finally consented to put on the clothes of the old
witch of Brentford, which happened to be upstairs.
Thus ingloriously disguised, he had taken a sound
beating at the hands of the man he meant to wrong,
and had retreated in cowardly haste.

Mrs Page said she would have the cudgel hallowed
and hung over the altar, so pleased was she that the
culprit had got his deserts. 'What think you?' said
Mrs Ford. 'May we, with warrant of womanhood and
the witness of a good conscience, pursue him with
any further revenge?' Mrs Page thought that the spirit

of wantonness was surely scared out of him; but she agreed that they should tell their husbands, and if Ford and Page desired to afflict him any further, it would be well.

Ford was very contrite when he heard his wife's confession. He humbly asked her pardon, and vowed he would henceforth rather suspect the sun with cold than her with any wantonness. Then he and Page agreed that the good dames should make public sport with the old fat fellow once again, so that he might be taken in the act and disgraced for his offences.

It was planned that the merry wives should meet Sir John by appointment in the park at midnight. There was an old tale of Herne the hunter, who had been a keeper once in Windsor Forest, and who, through all the wintertime, at midnight, walked round about an oak, with great ragged horns, blasting the trees and taking the cattle, and shaking a chain in a most hideous and dreadful manner. Travellers feared mightily to walk at night by Herne's oak, as it was called, and thus after sundown it was a deserted place. This was the spot fixed upon for the meeting, and it was agreed that Falstaff should be asked to come thither dressed with huge horns on his head, like Herne the hunter. 'Then,' quoth Mrs Page, 'my daughter and my little son and three or four more of their growth shall be dressed like urchins, ouphes, and fairies in green and white, and shall carry lighted tapers on their heads and rattles in their hands; and when Falstaff, Mrs Ford, and I are newly met they shall come forth suddenly with some song. We two will feign cowardice and fly, while they shall encircle him about and pinch him, fairy-like, asking why he dares to profane their sacred paths at that hallowed hour.'

This being arranged, the plotters parted, Ford promising to go once again to the knight disguised as Brook and learn all his purpose, after Dame Quickly had invited him to the midnight meeting.

When Mistress Quickly, bent upon this mission, reached the Garter Inn, Sir John was in the taproom lamenting very bitterly over the cudgelling he had received from Ford. 'If it should come to the ear of the court,' growled he, 'how I had been transformed, they would melt me out of my fat, drop by drop, and liquor fishermen's boots with me. I warrant they would whip me with their fine wits till I were as crestfallen as a dried pear.' Dame Quickly coming suddenly upon him in this mood, he grew furious when she told her errand from the good ladies. 'I have suffered more for their sakes,' quoth he, 'than the villanous inconstancy of man is able to bear.' 'And have they not suffered?' asked Mistress Quickly, playing her part of injured innocence right well. 'Mistress Ford, good heart, is beaten black and blue.' 'What tell'st thou me of black and blue?' roared the bruised and suffering knight; and his troubles, moreover, had not ended with a beating, for he was like to be apprehended, he said, for the witch of Brentford, but that his admirable dexterity of wit and his counterfeiting the action of an old woman had delivered him from the knave constable. Thus he railed on, always boasting of his own good parts while he bemoaned the injuries that really resulted from their lack.

Dame Quickly soothed him as best she could, and, asking for more privacy that she might deliver her tidings, he invited her into his own chamber. There, at last, she prevailed with him to go to Herne's oak at midnight, promising to provide him a chain and a pair of horns. Then she departed, well pleased with her success, and inwardly full of mirth at the old rogue's simplicity.

And now came Mr Brook to see Sir John and to learn how his venture of the day before had prospered. The knight was full of promises for the future, for he felt a crying need of some of Brook's gold; but he was in a mighty rage about what had happened him, and desired nothing so much as revenge upon Ford, whom he vowed he would undo that night, for he pledged himself to deliver Ford's wife into Mr Brook's hand.

As the Windsor clock struck twelve through the thick foliage of the park, Sir John came stealthily under the trees to keep his appointment by Herne's oak. He was dressed like a hunter and had a great pair of buck's horns on his head, fastened in a close hood that covered his ears and met under his chin. He muttered encouraging words to himself as he stole forward, for he was sore afraid of the dark, in spite of his vain boasting and show of courage. As he neared the huge gnarled oak which was to be his trysting-place with Mrs Ford and Mrs Page, the former came forth from her concealment in the trees and greeted him with well-feigned affection. He would have taken her in his huge arms, but that she retreated from his embrace and told him that Mrs Page had come with her. 'Divide me like a bribe-buck; each take a haunch,' said he. 'As I am a true spirit, welcome!'

Just then there came a strange noise abroad, and the good wives pretended to be alarmed. 'What should this be?' asked Falstaff, frightened in very truth. 'Away, away!' cried the dames in a breath, running off as they called; and, in an instant, Sir John was surrounded by a fairy throng, with Sir Hugh Evans

171

as a satyr and Mrs Quickly and Pistol as attendant sprites. They began to circle around him singing weird songs and twitching their tapers about on their swaying heads.

'They are fairies,' quoth Sir John. 'He that speaks to them shall die;' and he lay down upon his face in craven fear; they meanwhile chanting in time to their tiptoe steps and pinching him or burning him now and again with their tapers.

When they had sufficiently worked their will with him, there was a sound of a hunter's horn, at which all vanished away, and the sorry old gallant slowly rose, took off his horns, and got upon his feet. He looked around in terror, and well he might, for at the instant came running forth Page and Ford, with their wives, who seized him just in time to prevent him from taking to his ungainly heels. They made game of his foolish pretensions to gallantry, and it slowly dawned upon him that he had really been the dupe of the honest wives whom he had tried so hard to injure. Then said he, 'I do begin to perceive that I am made an ass,' which was a truth most aptly expressed; and he continued: 'And these are not fairies? I was three or four times in the thought they were not, and yet the guiltiness of my mind and the sudden surprise of my powers drove the grossness of the foppery into a received belief. See now, how wit may be made a Jack-a-lent, when 'tis upon ill employment,' for he still believed in his wit, and was willing to blame its miscarriage upon any cause saving the right one of its dullness. He did not feel so much remorse for his sins as shame for his little wit, and, seeing this, Mrs Page said these honest words: 'Why, Sir John, do you think, though we would have thrust virtue out of our hearts by the head and shoulders, that ever any power could have made you our delight?'

'What, a hodge-pudding? A bag of flax?' said Ford, derisively; and Page, in his turn, called him 'old, cold, and withered, and as poor as Job'; whereupon the crestfallen knight acknowledged himself dejected, and gave himself up to them to work what punishment they would.

'Marry, sir, we'll bring you to Windsor, to one

Master Brook, that you have cozened of money,' said Ford, still smarting from the old knight's deceptions; but Page, with good-humoured forgetfulness of his evil designs, bid him come to his house and eat a posset, and thither all went the more merrily because suspicion and jealousy had been cured by good sport and fair humour.

7

MUCH ADO
ABOUT
NOTHING

INTRODUCTION

Light, fast, witty, but with the slightest hint of 'man's inhumanity to man'—*Much Ado About Nothing* is one of Shakespeare's most popular comedies. We love the banter and repartee between Beatrice and Benedict. We are intrigued by the under-motivated malice of Don John towards his brother and community. We are shocked by the poor treatment of the innocent Hero, wrongly accused of having dealings with a man on the night before her wedding. And we are relieved when the truth is revealed, justice is done, and the lovers are finally married.

The tale begins when Don Pedro, the Prince of

Aragon, arrives at Messina, on return from a war, along with several young men of high rank in his army, including Claudio, a lord of Florence, and the witty Benedick, a lord of Padua. They are welcomed by the governor of Messina, Leonato, who introduces them to his daughter, Hero, and niece, Beatrice. Claudio and Hero fall in love and, with the assistance of the Prince, an early date is fixed for their marriage; Benedick and Beatrice, on the other hand, fall to verbally sparring with each other, until each is made to believe that the other is in love with them. Into this otherwise happy scene steps the figure of Don John. Don John is the half-brother of Don Pedro and a melancholy discontented man who hates the Prince and who hates Claudio because he is the Prince's friend. In order to satisfy his malicious wish to make the Prince and Claudio unhappy, Don John resolves to prevent the marriage of Claudio and Hero, and he employs a serving-man, Borachio, who has been wooing Hero's attendant, Margaret, to have her dress in Hero's clothes at night and be seen talking to him from her lady's chamber window. Through this ruse, Don John convinces the Prince and Claudio that Hero is unfaithful. The Prince and Claudio, in anger, decide to disgrace Hero on her marriage day, and in doing so they precipitate her physical collapse. Although the men soon find out the truth of the matter through the apprehension and confession of Borachio, Hero has already been held out as dead by Leonato, on the advice of a wise old friar, and all

Claudio can do to make amends to Leonato is offer to marry a cousin of Hero's. When this 'cousin' is revealed to be Hero herself, there is general rejoicing, followed by the wedding of Claudio and Hero, alongside that of Benedict and Beatrice.

At the centre of the tale is the 'nothing' of the title. That 'nothing' in Elizabethan slang refers to nothing short of the 'nothing' which (in Hamlet's words) lies between a maid's legs. From the outset, then, we know that in this tale there will be 'much ado' about female sexuality. Shakespeare takes a characteristically broad-minded view of the matter: while the male characters view female chastity as being of the utmost importance, their reaction to the slightest perceived transgression (here, talking out of a window to a man) is presented as being so palpably disproportionate that it is hard to believe that Shakespeare was condoning it. The whole trauma which threatens to tear apart families and friendships arises from precisely this 'nothing'.

On a philosophical level, there is a further 'nothing' haunting the characters of the tale—the absence of a firm connection with objective reality which arises from the dominance of subjective interpretations of experience. Claudio, notably, is led astray on multiple occasions: first in mistaking Don Pedro's intentions (suspecting him of wooing Hero on his own behalf), next in mistaking Hero's fidelity (suspecting her of betraying him before their wedding), then in believing her to be dead, and finally in believing that the marriage that concludes the tale was with Hero's cousin rather than Hero herself. There is, in fact, almost no point in the story at which Claudio has a firm grasp on the objective situation. The subjective world can even, on occasion, displace the objective world entirely: for Benedict and Beatrice, for example, each falls in love with the other through the mistaken belief that the other one is in love with them.

There is one final existential 'nothing' that manifests in the figure of the villain, Don John. Don John is the brother of Don Pedro and a bastard. It is Don John who hatches the plot to deceive Claudio and it is Don John who arranges its implementation. The troubling aspect of this is that Don John's malice appears to be—rather like Iago's malice in *Othello*—under-motivated: on his own account, Don John simply suggests that 'it must not be denied but I am a plain-dealing villain'. It is tempting to the modern reader to attribute this under-motivation either to an oversight on the part of the playwright or to the dramatic norms of the period. The difficulty with these explanations is that Shakespeare, like other dramatists of his generation, is demonstrably and self-evidently able to depict character in its most subtle delineations. More likely, if more troubling, is the alternative view: that there is darkness and malice in nature; they need no reason to exist, nor reason to act, and can strike at any moment without the slightest compunction.

MUCH ADO ABOUT NOTHING

There lived in the palace at Messina two ladies, whose names were Hero and Beatrice. Hero was the daughter, and Beatrice the niece, of Leonato, the governor of Messina.

Beatrice was of a lively temper, and loved to divert her cousin Hero, who was of a more serious disposition, with her sprightly sallies. Whatever was going forward was sure to make matter of mirth for the light-hearted Beatrice.

At the time the history of these ladies commences some young men of high rank in the army, as they were passing through Messina on their return from a war that was just ended, in which they had distinguished themselves by their great bravery, came to visit Leonato. Among these were Don Pedro, the Prince of Aragon; and his friend Claudio, who was a lord of Florence; and with them came the wild and witty Benedick, and he was a lord of Padua.

These strangers had been at Messina before, and the hospitable governor introduced them to his daughter and his niece as their old friends and acquaintance.

Benedick, the moment he entered the room, began a lively conversation with Leonato and the Prince. Beatrice, who liked not to be left out of any discourse, interrupted Benedick with saying: 'I wonder that you will still be talking, signior Benedick: nobody marks you.' Benedick was just such another rattle-brain as

179

Beatrice, yet he was not pleased at this free salutation; he thought it did not become a well-bred lady to be so flippant with her tongue; and he remembered, when he was last at Messina, that Beatrice used to select him to make her merry jests upon. And as there is no one who so little likes to be made a jest of as those who are apt to take the same liberty themselves, so it was with Benedick and Beatrice; these two sharp wits never met in former times but a perfect war of raillery was kept up between them, and they always parted mutually displeased with each other. Therefore when Beatrice stopped him in the middle of his discourse with telling him nobody marked what he was saying, Benedick, affecting not to have observed before that she was present, said: 'What, my dear lady Disdain, are you yet living?' And now war broke out afresh between them, and a long jangling argument ensued, during which Beatrice, although she knew he had so well approved his valour in the late war, said that she would eat all he had killed there; and observing the Prince take delight in Benedick's conversation, she called him 'the Prince's jester'. This sarcasm sunk deeper into the mind of Benedick than all Beatrice had said before. The hint she gave him that he was a coward, by saying she would eat all he had killed, he did not regard, knowing himself to be a brave man; but there is nothing that great wits so much dread as the imputation of buffoonery, because the charge comes sometimes a little too near the truth: therefore

Benedick perfectly hated Beatrice when she called him 'the Prince's jester'.

The modest Lady Hero was silent before the noble guests; and while Claudio was attentively observing the improvement which time had made in her beauty, and was contemplating the exquisite graces of her fine figure (for she was an admirable young lady), the Prince was highly amused with listening to the humorous dialogue between Benedick and Beatrice; and he said in a whisper to Leonato: 'This is a pleasant-spirited young lady. She were an excellent wife for Benedick.' Leonato replied to this suggestion: 'Oh, my lord, my lord, if they were but a week married, they would talk themselves mad.' But though Leonato thought they would make a discordant pair, the Prince did not give up the idea of matching these two keen wits together.

When the Prince returned with Claudio from the palace, he found that the marriage he had devised between Benedick and Beatrice was not the only one projected in that good company, for Claudio spoke in such terms of Hero as made the Prince guess at what was passing in his heart; and he liked it well, and he said to Claudio: 'Do you affect Hero?' To this question Claudio replied: 'O my lord, when I was last at Messina, I looked upon her with a soldier's eye, that liked, but had no leisure for loving; but now, in this happy time of peace, thoughts of war have left their places vacant in my mind, and in their room come thronging soft and delicate thoughts, all prompting me how fair young Hero is, reminding me that I liked her before I went to the wars.' Claudio's confession of his love for Hero so wrought upon the Prince, that he lost no time in soliciting the consent of Leonato to accept of Claudio for a son-in-law. Leonato agreed to this proposal, and the Prince found no great difficulty in persuading the gentle Hero herself to listen to the suit of the noble Claudio, who was a lord of rare endowments, and highly accomplished, and Claudio, assisted by his kind Prince, soon prevailed upon Leonato to fix an early day for the celebration of his marriage with Hero.

Claudio was to wait but a few days before he was

to be married to his fair lady; yet he complained of the interval being tedious, as indeed most young men are impatient when they are waiting for the accomplishment of any event they have set their hearts upon: the Prince, therefore, to make the time seem short to him, proposed as a kind of merry pastime that they should invent some artful scheme to make Benedick and Beatrice fall in love with each other. Claudio entered with great satisfaction into this whim of the Prince, and Leonato promised them his assistance, and even Hero said she would do any modest office to help her cousin to a good husband.

The device the Prince invented was that the gentlemen should make Benedick believe that Beatrice was in love with him, and that Hero should make Beatrice believe that Benedick was in love with her.

The Prince, Leonato, and Claudio began their operations first; and watching upon an opportunity when Benedick was quietly seated reading in an arbour, the Prince and his assistants took their station among the trees behind the arbour, so near that Benedick could not choose but hear all they said; and after some careless talk the Prince said: 'Come hither, Leonato. What was it you told me the other day—that your niece Beatrice was in love with signior Benedick? I did never think that lady would have loved any man.' 'No, nor I neither, my lord,' answered Leonato. 'It is most wonderful that she should so dote on Benedick, whom she in all outward behaviour seemed ever to dislike.' Claudio confirmed all this with saying that Hero had told him Beatrice was so in love with Benedick, that she would certainly die of grief if he could not be brought to love her; which Leonato and Claudio seemed to agree was impossible, he having always been such a railer against all fair ladies, and in particular against Beatrice.

The Prince affected to hearken to all this with great compassion for Beatrice, and he said: 'It were good that Benedick were told of this.' 'To what end?' said Claudio. 'He would but make sport of it, and torment the poor lady worse.' 'And if he should,' said the Prince, 'it were a good deed to hang him; for Beatrice is an excellent sweet lady, and exceeding wise in everything but in loving Benedick.' Then the Prince motioned to his companions that they should walk on, and leave Benedick to meditate upon what he had overheard.

Benedick had been listening with great eagerness to this conversation; and he said to himself when he heard Beatrice loved him: 'Is it possible? Sits the wind in that corner?' And when they were gone, he began to reason in this manner with himself. 'This can be no trick! They were very serious, and they have the truth from Hero, and seem to pity the lady. Love me! Why it must be requited! I did never think to marry. But when I said I should die a bachelor, I did not think I should live to be married. They say the lady is virtuous and fair. She is so. And wise in everything but loving me. Why, that is no great argument of her folly. But here comes Beatrice. By this day, she is a fair lady. I do spy some marks of love in her.' Beatrice now approached him, and said with her usual tartness: 'Against my will I am sent to bid you come in to dinner.' Benedick, who never felt himself disposed to speak so politely to her before, replied: 'Fair Beatrice, I thank you for your pains'; and when Beatrice, after two or three more rude speeches, left him, Benedick thought he observed a concealed meaning of kindness under the uncivil words she uttered, and he said aloud: 'If I do not take pity on her, I am a villain. If I do not love her, I am a Jew. I will go get her picture.'

The gentleman being thus caught in the net they had spread for him, it was now Hero's turn to play her part with Beatrice; and for this purpose she sent for Ursula and Margaret, two gentlewomen who attended upon her, and she said to Margaret: 'Good Margaret, run to the parlour; there you will find my cousin Beatrice talking with the Prince and Claudio. Whisper in her ear that I and Ursula are walking in the orchard, and that our discourse is all of her. Bid her steal into that pleasant arbour, where honeysuckles, ripened by the sun, like ungrateful minions, forbid the sun to enter.' This arbour, into which Hero desired Margaret to entice Beatrice, was the very same pleasant arbour where Benedick had so lately been an attentive listener.

'I will make her come, I warrant, presently,' said Margaret.

Hero, then taking Ursula with her into the orchard, said to her: 'Now, Ursula, when Beatrice comes, we will walk up and down this alley, and our talk must be only of Benedick, and when I name him, let it be your part to praise him more than ever man did merit. My talk to you must be how Benedick is in love with Beatrice. Now begin; for look where Beatrice like a lapwing runs close by the ground to hear our conference.' They then began; Hero saying, as if in answer to something which Ursula had said: 'No, truly, Ursula. She is too disdainful; her spirits are as coy as wild birds of the rock.' 'But are you sure,' said Ursula, 'that Benedick loves Beatrice so entirely?'

Hero replied: 'So says the Prince, and my lord Claudio, and they entreated me to acquaint her with it; but I persuaded them, if they loved Benedick, never to let Beatrice know of it.' 'Certainly,' replied Ursula, 'it were not good she knew his love, lest she made sport of it.' 'Why, to say truth,' said Hero, 'I never yet saw a man, how wise soever, or noble, young, or rarely featured, but she would dispraise him.' 'Sure, sure, such carping is not commendable,' said Ursula. 'No,' replied Hero, 'but who dare tell her so? If I should speak, she would mock me into air.' 'O! You wrong your cousin,' said Ursula. 'She cannot be so much without true judgment as to refuse so rare a gentleman as signior Benedick.' 'He hath an excellent good name,' said Hero. 'Indeed, he is the first man in Italy, always excepting my dear Claudio.' And now, Hero giving her attendant a hint that it was time to change the discourse, Ursula said: 'And when are you to be married, madam?' Hero then told her, that she was to be married to Claudio the next day, and desired she would go in with her, and look at some new attire, as she wished to consult with her on what she would wear on the morrow. Beatrice, who had been listening with breathless eagerness to this dialogue, when they went away, exclaimed: 'What fire is in mine ears? Can this be true? Farewell, contempt and scorn, and maiden pride, adieu! Benedick, love on! I will requite you, taming my wild heart to your loving hand.'

It must have been a pleasant sight to see these old enemies converted into new and loving friends, and to behold their first meeting after being cheated into mutual liking by the merry artifice of the good-humoured Prince. But a sad reverse in the fortunes of Hero must now be thought of. The morrow, which was to have been her wedding day, brought sorrow on the heart of Hero and her good father Leonato.

The Prince had a half-brother, who came from the wars along with him to Messina. This brother (his name was Don John) was a melancholy, discontented man, whose spirits seemed to labour in the contriving of villainies. He hated the Prince his brother, and he hated Claudio, because he was the Prince's friend, and determined to prevent Claudio's marriage with Hero, only for the malicious pleasure of making Claudio and the Prince unhappy; for he knew the Prince had set his heart upon this marriage, almost as much as Claudio himself; and to effect this wicked purpose, he employed one Borachio, a man as bad as himself, whom he encouraged with the offer of a great reward. This Borachio paid his court to Margaret, Hero's attendant; and Don John, knowing this, prevailed upon him to make Margaret promise to talk with him from her lady's chamber window that night, after Hero was asleep, and also to dress herself in Hero's clothes, the better to deceive Claudio into the belief that it was Hero; for that was the end he meant to compass by this wicked plot.

Don John then went to the Prince and Claudio, and told them that Hero was an imprudent lady, and that she talked with men from her chamber window at midnight. Now this was the evening before the wedding, and he offered to take them that night, where they should themselves hear Hero discoursing with a man from her window; and they consented to go along with him, and Claudio said: 'If I see anything tonight why I should not marry her, tomorrow in the congregation, where I intended to wed her, there will I shame her.' The Prince also said: 'And as I assisted you to obtain her, I will join with you to disgrace her.'

When Don John brought them near Hero's chamber that night, they saw Borachio standing under the window, and they saw Margaret looking out of Hero's window, and heard her talking with Borachio; and Margaret being dressed in the same clothes they had seen Hero wear, the Prince and Claudio believed it was the lady Hero herself.

Nothing could equal the anger of Claudio, when

he had made (as he thought) this discovery. All his love for the innocent Hero was at once converted into hatred, and he resolved to expose her in the church, as he had said he would, the next day; and the Prince agreed to this, thinking no punishment could be too severe for the naughty lady, who talked with a man from her window the very night before she was going to be married to the noble Claudio.

The next day, when they were all met to celebrate the marriage, and Claudio and Hero were standing before the priest, and the priest, or friar, as he was called, was proceeding to pronounce the marriage ceremony, Claudio, in the most passionate language, proclaimed the guilt of the blameless Hero, who, amazed at the strange words he uttered, said meekly: 'Is my lord well, that he does speak so wide?'

Leonato, in the utmost horror, said to the Prince: 'My lord, why speak not you?' 'What should I speak?' said the Prince. 'I stand dishonoured, that have gone about to link my dear friend to an unworthy woman. Leonato, upon my honour, myself, my brother, and this grieved Claudio, did see and hear her last night at midnight talk with a man at her chamber window.'

Benedick, in astonishment at what he heard, said: 'This looks not like a nuptial.'

'True, O God!' replied the heart-struck Hero; and then this hapless lady sunk down in a fainting fit, to all appearance dead. The Prince and Claudio left the church, without staying to see if Hero would recover, or at all regarding the distress into which they had thrown Leonato, so hard-hearted had their anger made them.

Benedick remained, and assisted Beatrice to recover Hero from her swoon, saying: 'How does the lady?' 'Dead, I think,' replied Beatrice in great agony, for she loved her cousin; and knowing her virtuous principles, she believed nothing of what she had heard spoken against her. Not so the poor old father; he believed the story of his child's shame, and it was piteous to hear him lamenting over her, as she lay like one dead before him, wishing she might never more open her eyes.

But the ancient friar was a wise man, and full of observation on human nature, and he had attentively marked the lady's countenance when she heard herself accused, and noted a thousand blushing shames to start into her face, and then he saw an angel-like whiteness bear away those blushes, and in her eye he saw a fire that did belie the error that the Prince did speak against her maiden truth, and he said to the sorrowing father: 'Call me a fool; trust not my reading, nor my observation; trust not my age, my reverence, nor my calling, if this sweet lady lie not guiltless here under some biting error.'

When Hero had recovered from the swoon into which she had fallen, the friar said to her: 'Lady, what man is he you are accused of?' Hero replied: 'They know that do accuse me; I know of none'; then turning to Leonato, she said: 'O my father, if you can prove that any man has ever conversed with me at hours unmeet, or that I yesternight changed words with any creature, refuse me, hate me, torture me to death.'

'There is,' said the friar, 'some strange misunderstanding in the Prince and Claudio'; and then he counselled Leonato, that he should report that Hero was dead; and he said that the death-like swoon in which they had left Hero would make this easy of belief; and he also advised him that he should put on mourning, and erect a monument for her, and do all rites that appertain to a burial. 'What shall become of this?' said Leonato. 'What will this do?' The friar replied: 'This report of her death shall change slander into pity: that is some good; but that is not all the good I hope for. When Claudio shall hear she died upon hearing his words, the idea of her life shall sweetly creep into his imagination. Then shall he mourn, if ever love had interest in his heart, and wish that he had not so accused her; yea, though he thought his accusation true.'

Benedick now said: 'Leonato, let the friar advise you; and though you know how well I love the Prince and Claudio, yet on my honour I will not reveal this secret to them.'

Leonato, thus persuaded, yielded; and he said sorrowfully: 'I am so grieved, that the smallest twine may lead me.' The kind friar then led Leonato and Hero away to comfort and console them, and Beatrice and Benedick remained alone; and this was the meeting from which their friends, who contrived the merry plot against them, expected so much diversion; those friends who were now overwhelmed with affliction, and from whose minds all thoughts of merriment seemed forever banished.

Benedick was the first who spoke, and he said: 'Lady Beatrice, have you wept all this while?' 'Yea, and I will weep a while longer,' said Beatrice. 'Surely,' said Benedick, 'I do believe your fair cousin is wronged.' 'Ah!' said Beatrice, 'how much might that man deserve of me who would right her!' Benedick then said: 'Is there any way to show such friendship? I do love nothing in the world so well as you: is not that strange?' 'It were as possible,' said Beatrice, 'for me to say I loved nothing in the world so well as you; but believe me not, and yet I lie not. I confess nothing, nor I deny nothing. I am sorry for my cousin.' 'By my sword,' said Benedick, 'You love me, and I protest I love you. Come, bid me do anything for you.' 'Kill Claudio,' said Beatrice. 'Ha! Not for the wide world,' said Benedick; for he loved his friend Claudio, and he believed he had been imposed upon. 'Is not Claudio a villain, that has slandered, scorned, and dishonoured my cousin?' said Beatrice. 'O that I were a man!' 'Hear me, Beatrice!' said Benedick. But Beatrice would hear nothing in Claudio's defence, and she continued to urge on Benedick to revenge her cousin's wrongs; and she said: 'Talk with a man out of the window; a proper saying! Sweet Hero! She is wronged; she is slandered; she is undone. O that I were a man for Claudio's sake! Or that I had any friend, who would be a man for my sake! But valour is melted into courtesies and compliments. I cannot be a man with wishing, therefore I will die a woman with grieving.'

'Tarry, good Beatrice,' said Benedick. 'By this hand I love you.' 'Use it for my love some other way than swearing by it,' said Beatrice. 'Think you on your soul that Claudio has wronged Hero?' asked Benedick. 'Yea,' answered Beatrice, 'as sure as I have a thought, or a soul.' 'Enough,' said Benedick. 'I am engaged; I will challenge him. I will kiss your hand, and so leave you. By this hand, Claudio shall render me a dear account! As you hear from me, so think of me. Go, comfort your cousin.'

While Beatrice was thus powerfully pleading with Benedick, and working his gallant temper by the spirit of her angry words to engage in the cause of Hero, and fight even with his dear friend Claudio, Leonato was challenging the Prince and Claudio to answer with their swords the injury they had done his child, who, he affirmed, had died for grief. But they respected his age and his sorrow, and they said: 'Nay, do not quarrel with us, good old man.' And now came Benedick, and he also challenged Claudio to answer with his sword the injury he had done to Hero; and Claudio and the Prince said to each other: 'Beatrice has set him on to do this.' Claudio nevertheless must have accepted this challenge of Benedick, had not the justice of Heaven at the moment brought to pass a better proof of the innocence of Hero than the uncertain fortune of a duel.

While the Prince and Claudio were yet talking of the challenge of Benedick, a magistrate brought Borachio as a prisoner before the Prince. Borachio had been overheard talking with one of his companions of the mischief he had been employed by Don John to do.

Borachio made a full confession to the Prince, in Claudio's hearing, that it was Margaret dressed in her lady's clothes that he had talked with from the window, whom they had mistaken for the lady Hero herself; and no doubt continued on the minds of Claudio and the Prince of the innocence of Hero. If a suspicion had remained it must have been removed by the flight of Don John, who, finding his villainies were detected, fled from Messina to avoid the just anger of his brother.

The heart of Claudio was sorely grieved when he found he had falsely accused Hero, who, he thought, died upon hearing his cruel words; and the memory of his beloved Hero's image came over him, in the rare semblance that he loved it first; and the Prince asking him if what he heard did not run like iron through his soul, he answered, that he felt as if he had taken poison while Borachio was speaking.

And the repentant Claudio implored forgiveness of the old man Leonato for the injury he had done his child; and promised, that whatever penance Leonato would lay upon him for his fault in believing the false accusation against his betrothed wife, for her dear sake he would endure it.

The penance Leonato enjoined him was to marry the next morning a cousin of Hero's, who, he said, was now his heir, and in person very like Hero. Claudio, regarding the solemn promise he made to Leonato, said, he would marry this unknown lady, even though she were an Ethiop; but his heart was very sorrowful, and he passed that night in tears, and in remorseful grief, at the tomb which Leonato had erected for Hero.

When the morning came, the Prince accompanied Claudio to the church, where the good friar, and Leonato and his niece, were already assembled to celebrate a second nuptial; and Leonato presented to Claudio his promised bride; and she wore a mask, that Claudio might not discover her face. And Claudio said to the lady in the mask: 'Give me your hand, before this holy friar; I am your husband, if you will marry me.' 'And when I lived I was your other wife,' said this unknown lady; and, taking off her mask, she proved to be no niece (as was pretended), but Leonato's very daughter, the lady Hero herself.

We may be sure that this proved a most agreeable surprise to Claudio, who thought her dead, so that he could scarcely for joy believe his eyes; and the Prince, who was equally amazed at what he saw, exclaimed: 'Is not this Hero, Hero that was dead?' Leonato replied: 'She died, my lord, but while her slander lived.' The friar promised them an explanation of this seeming miracle after the ceremony was ended; and was proceeding to marry them, when he was interrupted by Benedick, who desired to be married at the same time to Beatrice. Beatrice making some demur to this match, and Benedick challenging her with her love for him, which he had learned from Hero, a pleasant explanation took place; and they found, they had both been tricked into a belief of love, which had never existed, and had become lovers in truth by the power of a false jest; but the affection, which a merry invention had cheated them into, was grown too powerful to be shaken by a serious explanation; and since Benedick proposed to marry, he was resolved to think nothing to the purpose that the world could say against it, and he merrily kept up the jest, and swore to Beatrice that he took her but for pity, and because he heard she was dying of love for him; and Beatrice protested that she yielded but upon great persuasion, and partly to save his life, for she heard he was in a consumption. So these two mad wits were reconciled, and made a match of it, after Claudio and Hero were married; and to complete the history, Don John, the contriver of the villainy, was taken in his flight, and brought back to Messina; and a brave punishment it was to this gloomy, discontented man, to see the joy and feastings which, by the disappointment of his plots, took place in the palace in Messina.

8

AS YOU LIKE IT

INTRODUCTION

The clue to what *As You Like It* is about is in its title.

It is often said that Shakespeare chose this title because it was conventional for Elizabethan playwrights to beg their audience's indulgence. Indeed, at the end of the play, Shakespeare (through the figure of Rosalind) does just that, urging the women in the audience 'for the love you bear to men, to like as much of this play as please you' and for the men to do likewise. Sometimes it is even suggested that Shakespeare was aware he had written little more than a crowdpleaser, and that the title merely reflects that.

Let's consider, however, the possibility that Shakespeare may be communicating something more philosophical: the idea that the most effective posture towards life is one of positive embrace of one's destiny. In this context, 'as you like it' means not only 'as you please' but also connotes, more profoundly, 'so be it'.

The tale is set in an unspecified province of France where a usurper, Frederick, has deposed and banished his elder brother. Frederick's brother, the lawful Duke, retreats with his faithful followers into the forest of Arden, where they establish a community of exiles. Frederick's daughter, Celia, and his niece, Rosalind, remain in Fredrick's court, but, conscious that Rosalind is the rightful Duke's daughter, Frederick soon banishes her too. Rosalind and Celia flee to Arden to join the exiled Duke disguised, respectively, as young countryman and country lass, Rosalind taking the name Ganymede and Celia the name Aliena. It so happens that Orlando, with whom Rosalind has fallen in love, has also fled to Arden, in his case to avoid the wrath and predations of an envious elder brother, Oliver. Rosalind discovers that Orlando, still lovestruck, has been misspending his time carving Rosalind's name in trees and fastening love poems to them, prompting Rosalind (disguised as Ganymede) to propose a remedy—namely, that Orlando woo Ganymede as he would do Rosalind, in order that he be made ashamed of his love. Ultimately, both Frederick and Oliver, coming to the forest, repent their wrongdoings, Rosalind and Celia are married to Orlando and Oliver respectively, and the exiles return to the palace of the lawful Duke.

What the tale highlights is the futility of constantly grasping for what you don't have. Frederick grasps—and his reward is the loss of a brother, daughter, and niece. Oliver grasps—and his reward is the loss of a brother and faithful servant. Even putting to one side the practical futility of all this striving, consider for a moment its psychological consequences. There is a revealing moment when the usurping Frederick addresses his daughter Celia about her cousin (and Frederick's niece) Rosalind. 'She is too subtle for you; her smoothness, her very silence, and her patience speak to the people, and they pity her,' he says. 'You are a fool to plead for her, for you will seem more bright and virtuous when she is gone.' There is no need for Shakespeare to elaborate on the consequences of such thoughts. Their logic leads in one direction and one direction alone: towards the driving out of all that is good in one's environment for fear of being eclipsed by it.

In stark contrast is the forest of Arden to which the refugees from the striving world retreat. Arden has a quasi-mystical significance: it is a place of sanctuary, healing, and redemption. The source of this healing is the total acceptance and gratitude that characterize its most noteworthy inhabitants. The words of the exiled Duke capture the very essence of the tale: 'I find that howsoever men speak against adversity,' he says, 'yet some sweet uses are to be extracted from it; like the jewel, precious for medicine, which is taken from the head of the venomous and despised toad.' It is telling that Arden offers succour precisely to those who are most exhausted and most on the brink of giving up hope. In doing so, the tale charts a well-defined psychological journey from entanglement with the ways of the world, to exhaustion, disillusionment and despair, and out again on the other side to a state of wise forbearance and joy.

Even the love affair between Orlando and Rosalind bears its own mystical significance. From where we stand now, it is tempting to look on at the curious scene of a boy (Orlando) wooing a boy pretending to be a girl (the boy actor playing Rosalind) pretending to be a boy (Rosalind playing the role of the boy Ganymede) as an early modern anticipation of our era's own sexual values. But the significance is deeper than that. For what the tale really displays is Orlando at all times in the presence of the very object of his desire without knowing it. And there we have the great message for life that Shakespeare has so successfully communicated in *As You Like It*: that what we struggle and strive for is often that which has been before our very eyes all along.

AS YOU LIKE IT

During the time that France was divided into provinces (or dukedoms as they were called) there reigned in one of these provinces a usurper, who had deposed and banished his elder brother, the lawful Duke.

The Duke, who was thus driven from his dominions, retired with a few faithful followers to the forest of Arden; and here the good Duke lived with his loving friends, who had put themselves into a voluntary exile for his sake, while their land and revenues enriched the false usurper; and custom soon made the life of careless ease they led here more sweet to them than the pomp and uneasy splendour of a courtier's life. Here they lived like the old Robin Hood of England, and to this forest many noble youths daily resorted from the court, and did fleet the time carelessly, as they did who lived in the golden age. In the summer they lay along under the fine shade of the large forest trees, marking the playful sports of the wild deer; and so fond were they of these poor dappled fools, who seemed to be the native inhabitants of the forest, that it grieved them to be forced to kill them to supply themselves with venison for their food.

When the cold winds of winter made the Duke feel the change of his adverse fortune, he would endure it patiently, and say: 'These chilling winds which blow upon my body are true counsellors; they do not flatter, but represent truly to me my condition; and though they bite sharply, their tooth is nothing like so keen as that of unkindness and ingratitude. I find that howsoever men speak against adversity, yet some sweet uses are to be extracted from it; like the jewel, precious for medicine, which is taken from the head of the venomous and despised toad.' In this manner did the patient Duke draw a useful moral from everything that he saw; and by the help of this moralizing turn, in that life of his, remote from public haunts, he could find tongues in trees, books in the running brooks, sermons in stones, and good in everything.

The banished Duke had an only daughter, named Rosalind, whom the usurper, Duke Frederick, when he banished her father, still retained in his court as a companion for his own daughter Celia. A strict friendship subsisted between these ladies, which the disagreement between their fathers did not in the least interrupt, Celia striving by every kindness in her power to make amends to Rosalind for the injustice of her own father in deposing the father of Rosalind; and whenever the thoughts of her father's banishment, and her own dependence on the false usurper, made Rosalind melancholy, Celia's whole care was to comfort and console her.

One day, when Celia was talking in her usual kind

manner to Rosalind, saying, 'I pray you, Rosalind, my sweet cousin, be merry,' a messenger entered from the Duke, to tell them that if they wished to see a wrestling match, which was just going to begin, they must come instantly to the court before the palace; and Celia, thinking it would amuse Rosalind, agreed to go and see it.

In those times wrestling, which is only practised now by country clowns, was a favourite sport even in the courts of princes, and before fair ladies and princesses. To this wrestling match, therefore, Celia and Rosalind went. They found that it was likely to prove a very tragical sight; for a large and powerful man, who had been long practised in the art of wrestling, and had slain many men in contests of this kind, was just going to wrestle with a very young man, who, from his extreme youth and inexperience in the art, the beholders all thought would certainly be killed.

When the Duke saw Celia and Rosalind, he said: 'How now, daughter and niece, are you crept hither to see the wrestling? You will take little delight in it, there is such odds in the men: in pity to this young man, I would wish to persuade him from wrestling. Speak to him, ladies, and see if you can move him.'

The ladies were well pleased to perform this humane office, and first Celia entreated the young stranger that he would desist from the attempt; and then Rosalind spoke so kindly to him, and with such feeling consideration for the danger he was about to undergo, that instead of being persuaded by her gentle words to forgo his purpose, all his thoughts were bent to distinguish himself by his courage in this lovely lady's eyes. He refused the request of Celia and Rosalind in such graceful and modest words that they felt still more concern for him; he concluded his refusal with saying: 'I am sorry to deny such fair and excellent ladies anything. But let your fair eyes and gentle wishes go with me to my trial, wherein if I be conquered there is one shamed that was never gracious; if I am killed, there is one dead that is willing to die; I shall do my friends no wrong, for I have none to lament me; the world no injury, for in it I have nothing; for I only fill up a place in the world which may be better supplied when I have made it empty.'

And now the wrestling match began. Celia wished the young stranger might not be hurt; but Rosalind felt most for him. The friendless state which he said he was in, and that he wished to die, made Rosalind think that he was like herself, unfortunate; and she pitied him so much, and so deep an interest she took in his danger while he was wrestling, that she might almost be said at that moment to have fallen in love with him.

The kindness shown this unknown youth by these fair and noble ladies gave him courage and strength, so that he performed wonders; and in the end completely conquered his antagonist, who was so much hurt, that for a while he was unable to speak or move.

The Duke Frederick was much pleased with the courage and skill shown by this young stranger; and desired to know his name and parentage, meaning to take him under his protection.

The stranger said his name was Orlando, and that he was the youngest son of Sir Rowland de Boys.

Sir Rowland de Boys, the father of Orlando, had been dead some years; but when he was living, he had been a true subject and dear friend of the banished Duke; therefore, when Frederick heard Orlando was the son of his banished brother's friend, all his liking for this brave young man was changed into displeasure, and he left the place in very ill humour. Hating to hear the very name of any of his brother's friends, and yet still admiring the valour of the youth, he said, as he went out, that he wished Orlando had been the son of any other man.

Rosalind was delighted to hear that her new favourite was the son of her father's old friend; and she said to Celia: 'My father loved Sir Rowland de Boys, and if I had known this young man was his son, I would have added tears to my entreaties before he should have ventured.'

The ladies then went up to him; and seeing him abashed by the sudden displeasure shown by the Duke, they spoke kind and encouraging words to him; and Rosalind, when they were going away, turned back to speak some more civil things to the brave young son of her father's old friend; and taking a chain from off her neck, she said: 'Gentleman, wear this for me. I am out of suits with fortune, or I would give you a more valuable present.'

When the ladies were alone, Rosalind's talk being still of Orlando, Celia began to perceive her cousin had fallen in love with the handsome young wrestler, and she said to Rosalind: 'Is it possible you should fall in love so suddenly?' Rosalind replied: 'The Duke, my father, loved his father dearly.' 'But,' said Celia, 'does it therefore follow that you should love his son dearly? For then I ought to hate him, for my father hated his father; yet I do not hate Orlando.'

Frederick being enraged at the sight of Sir Rowland de Boys' son, which reminded him of the many friends the banished Duke had among the nobility, and having been for some time displeased with his niece, because the people praised her for her virtues, and pitied her for her good father's sake, his malice suddenly broke out against her; and while Celia and Rosalind were talking of Orlando, Frederick entered the room, and with looks full of anger ordered Rosalind instantly to leave the palace, and follow her father into banishment; telling Celia, who in vain pleaded for her, that he had only suffered Rosalind to stay upon her account. 'I did not then,' said Celia, 'entreat you to let her stay, for I was too young at that time to value her; but now that I know her worth, and that we so long have slept together, rose at the same instant, learned, played, and eat together, I cannot live out of her company.' Frederick replied: 'She is too subtle for you; her smoothness, her very silence, and her patience speak to the people, and they pity her. You are a fool to plead for her, for you will seem more bright and virtuous when she is gone; therefore open not your lips in her favour, for the doom which I have passed upon her is irrevocable.'

When Celia found she could not prevail upon her father to let Rosalind remain with her, she generously resolved to accompany her; and leaving her father's palace that night, she went along with her friend to seek Rosalind's father, the banished Duke, in the forest of Arden.

Before they set out, Celia considered that it would be unsafe for two young ladies to travel in the rich clothes they then wore; she therefore proposed that they should disguise their rank by dressing themselves like country maids. Rosalind said it would be a still greater protection if one of them was to be dressed like a man; and so it was quickly agreed on between them, that as Rosalind was the tallest, she should wear the dress of a young countryman, and Celia should be habited like a country lass, and that they should say they were brother and sister, and Rosalind said she would be called Ganymede, and Celia chose the name of Aliena.

In this disguise, and taking their money and jewels to defray their expenses, these fair princesses set out on their long travel; for the forest of Arden was a long way off, beyond the boundaries of the Duke's dominions.

The Lady Rosalind (or Ganymede as she must now

be called) with her manly garb seemed to have put on a manly courage. The faithful friendship Celia had shown in accompanying Rosalind so many weary miles made the new brother, in recompense for this true love, exert a cheerful spirit, as if he were indeed Ganymede, the rustic and stout-hearted brother of the gentle village maiden, Aliena.

When at last they came to the forest of Arden, they no longer found the convenient inns and good accommodations they had met with on the road; and being in want of food and rest, Ganymede, who had so merrily cheered his sister with pleasant speeches and happy remarks all the way, now owned to Aliena that he was so weary, he could find in his heart to disgrace his man's apparel, and cry like a woman; and Aliena declared she could go no farther; and then again Ganymede tried to recollect that it was a man's duty to comfort and console a woman, as the weaker vessel; and to seem courageous to his new sister; he said: 'Come, have a good heart, my sister Aliena; we are now, at the end of our travel, in the forest of Arden.' But feigned manliness and forced courage would no longer support them; for though they were in the forest of Arden, they knew not where to find the Duke; and here the travel of these weary ladies might have come to a sad conclusion, for they might have lost themselves, and perished for want of food; but providentially, as they were sitting on the grass, almost dying with fatigue and hopeless of any relief, a countryman chanced to pass that way, and Ganymede once more tried to speak with a manly boldness, saying: 'Shepherd, if love or gold can in this desert place procure us entertainment, I pray you bring us where we may rest ourselves; for this young maid, my sister, is much fatigued with travelling, and faints for want of food.'

The man replied that he was only a servant to a shepherd, and that his master's house was just going to be sold, and therefore they would find but poor entertainment; but that if they would go with him, they should be welcome to what there was. They followed the man, the near prospect of relief giving them fresh strength; and bought the house and sheep of the shepherd, and took the man who conducted them to the shepherd's house to wait on them; and being by this means so fortunately provided with a neat cottage, and well supplied with provisions, they agreed to stay here till they could learn in what part of the forest the Duke dwelt.

When they were rested after the fatigue of their journey, they began to like their new way of life, and almost fancied themselves the shepherd and shepherdess they feigned to be: yet sometimes Ganymede remembered he had once been the same Lady Rosalind who had so dearly loved the brave Orlando, because he was the son of old Sir Rowland, her father's friend; and though Ganymede thought that Orlando was many miles distant, even so many weary miles as they had travelled, yet it soon appeared that Orlando was also in the forest of Arden; and in this manner this strange event came to pass.

Orlando was the youngest son of Sir Rowland de Boys, who, when he died, left him (Orlando being then very young) to the care of his eldest brother Oliver, charging Oliver on his blessing to give his brother a good education, and provide for him as became the dignity of their ancient house. Oliver proved an unworthy brother; and disregarding the commands of his dying father, he never put his brother to school, but kept him at home untaught and entirely neglected. But in his nature and in the noble qualities of his mind Orlando so much resembled his excellent father that without any advantages of education he seemed like a youth who had been bred with the utmost care; and Oliver so envied the fine person and dignified manners of his untutored brother, that at last he wished to destroy him; and to effect this he set on people to persuade him to wrestle with the famous wrestler who, as has been before related, had killed so many men. Now, it was this cruel brother's neglect of him which made Orlando say he wished to die, being so friendless.

When, contrary to the wicked hopes he had formed, his brother proved victorious, his envy and malice knew no bounds, and he swore he would burn the chamber where Orlando slept. He was overheard making this vow by one that had been an old and faithful servant to their father, and that loved Orlando because he resembled Sir Rowland. This old man went out to meet him when he returned from the Duke's palace, and when he saw Orlando, the peril his dear young master was in made him break out into these passionate exclamations: 'O my gentle master, my sweet master, O you memory of old Sir Rowland! Why are you virtuous? Why are you gentle, strong, and valiant? And why would you be so fond to overcome the famous wrestler? Your praise is come too swiftly home before you.' Orlando, wondering what all this meant, asked him what was the matter. And then the old man told him how his wicked brother, envying the love all people bore him, and now hearing the fame he had gained by his victory in the Duke's palace, intended to destroy him by setting fire to his chamber that night; and in conclusion, advised him to escape the danger he was in by instant flight; and knowing Orlando had no money, Adam (for that was the good old man's name) had brought out with him his own little hoard, and he said: 'I have five hundred crowns, the thrifty hire I saved under your father, and laid by to be provision for me when my old limbs should become unfit for service; take that, and He that doth the ravens feed be comfort to my age! Here is the gold; all this I give to you: let me be your servant; though I look old I will do the service of a younger man in all your business and necessities.' 'O good old man!' said Orlando, 'how well appears in you the constant service of the old world! You are not for the fashion of these times. We will go along together, and before your youthful wages are spent, I shall light upon some means for both our maintenance.'

Together then this faithful servant and his loved master set out; and Orlando and Adam travelled on, uncertain what course to pursue, till they came to the forest of Arden, and there they found themselves in the same distress for want of food that Ganymede and Aliena had been. They wandered on, seeking some human habitation, till they were almost spent with hunger and fatigue. Adam at last said: 'O my dear master, I die for want of food, I can go no farther!' He then laid himself down, thinking to make that place his grave, and bade his dear master farewell. Orlando, seeing him in this weak state, took his old servant up in his arms, and carried him under the shelter of some pleasant trees; and he said to him: 'Cheerly, old

Adam, rest your weary limbs here awhile, and do not talk of dying!'

Orlando then searched about to find some food, and he happened to arrive at that part of the forest where the Duke was; and he and his friends were just going to eat their dinner, this royal Duke being seated on the grass, under no other canopy than the shady covert of some large trees.

Orlando, whom hunger had made desperate, drew his sword, intending to take their meat by force, and said: 'Forbear and eat no more; I must have your food!' The Duke asked him if distress had made him so bold, or if he were a rude despiser of good manners? On this Orlando said he was dying with hunger; and then the Duke told him he was welcome to sit down and eat with them. Orlando hearing him speak so gently, put up his sword, and blushed with shame at the rude manner in which he had demanded their food. 'Pardon me, I pray you,' said he. 'I thought that all things had been savage here, and therefore I put on the countenance of stern command; but whatever men you are, that in this desert, under the shade of melancholy boughs, lose and neglect the creeping hours of time; if ever you have looked on better days; if ever you have been where bells have knolled to church; if you have ever sat at any good man's feast; if ever from your eyelids you have wiped a tear, and know what it is to pity or be pitied, may gentle speeches now move you to do me human courtesy!' The Duke replied: 'True it is that we are men (as you say) who have seen better days, and though we have now our habitation in this wild forest, we have lived in towns and cities, and have with holy bell been knolled to church, have sat at good men's feasts, and from our eyes have wiped the drops which sacred pity has engendered; therefore sit you down, and take of our refreshment as much as will minister to your wants.' 'There is an old poor man,' answered Orlando, 'who has limped after me many a weary step in pure love, oppressed at once with two sad infirmities, age and hunger; till he be satisfied, I must not touch a bit.' 'Go, find him out, and bring him hither,' said the Duke. 'We will forbear to eat till you return.' Then Orlando went like a doe to find its fawn and give it food; and presently returned, bringing Adam in his arms; and the Duke said: 'Set down your venerable burthen; you are both welcome'; and they fed the old man, and cheered his heart, and he revived, and recovered his health and strength again.

The Duke inquired who Orlando was; and when he found that he was the son of his old friend, Sir Rowland de Boys, he took him under his protection, and Orlando and his old servant lived with the Duke in the forest.

Orlando arrived in the forest not many days after Ganymede and Aliena came there, and (as has been before related) bought the shepherd's cottage.

Ganymede and Aliena were strangely surprised to find the name of Rosalind carved on the trees, and love sonnets fastened to them, all addressed to Rosalind; and while they were wondering how this could be, they met Orlando, and they perceived the chain which Rosalind had given him about his neck.

Orlando little thought that Ganymede was the fair princess Rosalind, who, by her noble condescension and favour, had so won his heart that he passed his whole time in carving her name upon the trees, and writing sonnets in praise of her beauty; but being much pleased with the graceful air of this pretty shepherd-youth, he entered into conversation with him, and he thought he saw a likeness in Ganymede to his beloved Rosalind, but that he had none of the dignified deportment of that noble lady; for Ganymede assumed the forward manners often seen in youths when they are between boys and men, and with much archness and humour talked to Orlando of a certain lover, 'who,' said he, 'haunts our forest, and spoils our young trees with carving Rosalind upon their barks; and he hangs odes upon hawthorns, and elegies on brambles, all praising this same Rosalind. If I could find this love, I would give him some good counsel that would soon cure him of his love.'

Orlando confessed that he was the fond lover of whom he spoke, and asked Ganymede to give him the good counsel he talked of. The remedy Ganymede proposed, and the counsel he gave him, was that Orlando should come every day to the cottage where he and his sister Aliena dwelt: 'And then,' said Ganymede, 'I will feign myself to be Rosalind, and you shall feign to court me in the same manner as you would do if I was Rosalind, and then I will imitate the fantastic ways of whimsical ladies to their lovers, till I make you ashamed of your love; and this is the way I propose to cure you.' Orlando had no great faith in the remedy, yet he agreed to come every day to Ganymede's cottage, and feign a playful courtship; and every day Orlando visited Ganymede and Aliena, and Orlando called the shepherd Ganymede his Rosalind, and every day talked over all the fine words and flattering compliments which young men delight to use when they court their mistresses. It does not appear, however, that Ganymede made any progress in curing Orlando of his love for Rosalind.

Though Orlando thought all this was but a sportive

play (not dreaming that Ganymede was his very Rosalind), yet the opportunity it gave him of saying all the fond things he had in his heart pleased his fancy almost as well as it did Ganymede's, who enjoyed the secret jest in knowing these fine love speeches were all addressed to the right person.

In this manner many days passed pleasantly on with these young people; and the good-natured Aliena, seeing it made Ganymede happy, let him have his own way, and was diverted at the mock courtship, and did not care to remind Ganymede that the Lady Rosalind had not yet made herself known to the Duke her father, whose place of resort in the forest they had learnt from Orlando. Ganymede met the Duke one day, and had some talk with him, and the Duke asked of what parentage he came. Ganymede answered that he came of as good parentage as he did, which made the Duke smile, for he did not suspect the pretty shepherd boy came of royal lineage. Then seeing the Duke look well and happy, Ganymede was content to put off all further explanation for a few days longer.

One morning, as Orlando was going to visit Ganymede, he saw a man lying asleep on the ground, and a large green snake had twisted itself about his neck. The snake, seeing Orlando approach, glided away among the bushes. Orlando went nearer, and then he discovered a lioness lie crouching with her head on the ground, with a cat-like watch, waiting until the sleeping man awaked (for it is said that lions will prey on nothing that is dead or sleeping). It seemed as if Orlando was sent by Providence to free the man from the danger of the snake and lioness; but when Orlando looked in the man's face, he perceived that the sleeper who was exposed to this double peril, was his own brother Oliver, who had so cruelly used him, and had threatened to destroy him by fire; and he was almost tempted to leave him a prey to the hungry lioness; but brotherly affection and the gentleness of his nature soon overcame his first anger against his brother; and he drew his sword, and attacked the lioness, and slew her, and thus preserved his brother's life both from the venomous snake and from the furious lioness; but before Orlando could conquer the lioness, she had torn one of his arms with her sharp claws.

While Orlando was engaged with the lioness, Oliver awaked, and perceiving that his brother

Orlando, whom he had so cruelly treated, was saving him from the fury of a wild beast at the risk of his own life, shame and remorse at once seized him, and he repented of his unworthy conduct, and besought with many tears his brother's pardon for the injuries he had done him. Orlando rejoiced to see him so penitent, and readily forgave him: they embraced each other; and from that hour Oliver loved Orlando with a true brotherly affection, though he had come to the forest bent on his destruction.

The wound in Orlando's arm having bled very much, he found himself too weak to go to visit Ganymede, and therefore he desired his brother to go and tell Ganymede, 'whom,' said Orlando, 'I in sport do call my Rosalind,' the accident which had befallen him.

Thither then Oliver went, and told to Ganymede and Aliena how Orlando had saved his life; and when he had finished the story of Orlando's bravery, and his own providential escape, he owned to them that he was Orlando's brother, who had so cruelly used him; and then he told them of their reconciliation.

The sincere sorrow that Oliver expressed for his offences made such a lively impression on the kind heart of Aliena, that she instantly fell in love with him; and Oliver observing how much she pitied the distress he told her he felt for his fault, he as suddenly fell in love with her. But while love was thus stealing into the hearts of Aliena and Oliver, he was no less busy with Ganymede, who hearing of the danger

Orlando had been in, and that he was wounded by the lioness, fainted; and when he recovered, he pretended that he had counterfeited the swoon in the imaginary character of Rosalind, and Ganymede said to Oliver: 'Tell your brother Orlando how well I counterfeited a swoon.' But Oliver saw by the paleness of his complexion that he did really faint, and much wondering at the weakness of the young man, he said: 'Well, if you did counterfeit, take a good heart, and counterfeit to be a man.' 'So I do,' replied Ganymede, truly, 'but I should have been a woman by right.'

Oliver made this visit a very long one, and when at last he returned back to his brother, he had much news to tell him; for besides the account of Ganymede's fainting at the hearing that Orlando was wounded, Oliver told him how he had fallen in love with the fair shepherdess Aliena, and that she had lent a favourable ear to his suit, even in this their first interview; and he talked to his brother, as of a thing almost settled, that he should marry Aliena, saying that he so well loved her that he would live here as a shepherd, and settle his estate and house at home upon Orlando.

'You have my consent,' said Orlando. 'Let your wedding be tomorrow, and I will invite the Duke and his friends. Go and persuade your shepherdess to this: she is now alone; for look, here comes her brother.' Oliver went to Aliena; and Ganymede, whom Orlando had perceived approaching, came to inquire after the health of his wounded friend.

When Orlando and Ganymede began to talk over the sudden love which had taken place between Oliver and Aliena, Orlando said he had advised his brother to persuade his fair shepherdess to be married on the morrow, and then he added how much he could wish to be married on the same day to his Rosalind.

Ganymede, who well approved of this arrangement, said that if Orlando really loved Rosalind as well as he professed to do, he should have his wish; for on the morrow he would engage to make Rosalind appear in her own person, and also that Rosalind should be willing to marry Orlando.

This seemingly wonderful event, which, as Ganymede was the Lady Rosalind, he could so easily perform, he pretended he would bring to pass by the aid of magic, which he said he had learnt of an uncle who was a famous magician.

The fond lover Orlando, half believing and half doubting what he heard, asked Ganymede if he spoke in sober meaning. 'By my life I do,' said Ganymede. 'Therefore put on your best clothes, and bid the Duke and your friends to your wedding; for if you desire to be married tomorrow to Rosalind, she shall be here.'

The next morning, Oliver having obtained the consent of Aliena, they came into the presence of the Duke, and with them also came Orlando.

They being all assembled to celebrate this double marriage, and as yet only one of the brides appearing, there was much of wondering and conjecture, but they mostly thought that Ganymede was making a jest of Orlando.

The Duke, hearing that it was his own daughter that was to be brought in this strange way, asked Orlando if he believed the shepherd boy could really do what he had promised; and while Orlando was answering that he knew not what to think, Ganymede entered, and asked the Duke, if he brought his daughter, whether he would consent to her marriage with Orlando. 'That I would,' said the Duke, 'if I had kingdoms to give with her.' Ganymede then said to Orlando: 'And you say you will marry her if I bring her here.' 'That I would,' said Orlando, 'if I were king of many kingdoms.'

Ganymede and Aliena then went out together, and Ganymede throwing off his male attire, and being once more dressed in woman's apparel, quickly became Rosalind without the power of magic; and Aliena changing her country garb for her own rich clothes, was with as little trouble transformed into the Lady Celia.

While they were gone, the Duke said to Orlando, that he thought the shepherd Ganymede very like his daughter Rosalind; and Orlando said he also had observed the resemblance.

They had no time to wonder how all this would end, for Rosalind and Celia in their own clothes entered; and no longer pretending that it was by the power of magic that she came there, Rosalind threw herself on her knees before her father and begged his blessing. It seemed so wonderful to all present that she should so suddenly appear that it might well have passed for magic; but Rosalind would no longer trifle with her father, and told him the story of her banishment, and of her dwelling in the forest as a shepherd boy, her cousin Celia passing as her sister.

The Duke ratified the consent he had already given to the marriage; and Orlando and Rosalind, Oliver and Celia, were married at the same time. And though their wedding could not be celebrated in this wild forest with any of the parade or splendour usual on such occasions, yet a happier wedding day was never passed; and while they were eating their venison under the cool shade of the pleasant trees, as if nothing should be wanting to complete the felicity of this good Duke and the true lovers, an unexpected messenger arrived to tell the Duke the joyful news that his dukedom was restored to him.

The usurper, enraged at the flight of his daughter Celia, and hearing that every day men of great worth resorted to the forest of Arden to join the lawful Duke in his exile, much envying that his brother should be so highly respected in his adversity, put himself at the head of a large force, and advanced towards the forest, intending to seize his brother, and put him with all his faithful followers to the sword; but, by a wonderful interposition of Providence, this bad brother was converted from his evil intention; for just as he entered the skirts of the wild forest, he was met by an old religious man, a hermit, with whom he had much talk, and who in the end completely turned his heart from his wicked design. Thenceforward he became a true penitent, and resolved, relinquishing his unjust dominion, to spend the remainder of his days in a religious house. The first act of his newly conceived penitence was to send a messenger to his brother (as has been related) to offer to restore to him his dukedom, which he had usurped so long, and with it the lands and revenues of his friends, the faithful followers of his adversity.

This joyful news, as unexpected as it was welcome, came opportunely to heighten the festivity and rejoicings at the wedding of the princesses. Celia complimented her cousin on this good fortune which had happened to the Duke, Rosalind's father, and wished her joy very sincerely, though she herself was no longer heir to the dukedom, but by this restoration which her father had made Rosalind was now the heir: so completely was the love of these two cousins unmixed with anything of jealousy or of envy.

The Duke had now an opportunity of rewarding those true friends who had stayed with him in his banishment; and these worthy followers, though they had patiently shared his adverse fortune, were very well pleased to return in peace and prosperity to the palace of their lawful Duke.

9

TWELFTH NIGHT, OR WHAT YOU WILL

INTRODUCTION

Twelfth Night is generally considered one of Shakespeare's most successful comedies. It is an alluring combination of romance, humour, and acute human and social observation.

The title, 'Twelfth Night', alludes to the festivities traditionally held on the twelfth night after Christmas—the climax of the festive season celebrated with music, masked balls, and unbridled revelry. Twelfth Night was, in particular, associated with 'misrule': the temporary inversion or breaking down of the social order marked by the ascension of a 'Lord of Misrule' who would preside over a topsy-turvy world until the festival came to an end at midnight.

The story itself begins when twin brother and sister, Sebastian and Viola, are shipwrecked on the coast of Illyria (now the Western Balkans). Afflicted by the loss of her brother, Viola takes on disguise as a boy in order to enter the service of the governor of Illyria, Orsino, under the name 'Cesario'. Orsino is desperately in love with a lady, Olivia, who resolutely rejects his approaches, and he enlists Cesario to act as his emissary. Olivia, however, proceeds to fall in love with Cesario rather than Orsino, just as Viola (still in disguise as Cesario) falls in love with Orsino. After a series of mishaps and mistaken identities, the true identity of Viola is revealed when her brother Sebastian arrives on the scene, leading to the marriage of Orsino with Viola, and Olivia with Sebastian.

The tale is about courtship and love: what works, what doesn't, and why. In *Twelfth Night*, Orsino adopts the role of the courtly lover in his courtship of Olivia, 'courtly love' being a highly conventional mode of courtship in which the lover was to devote himself to serving an idealized, unattainable, and unyielding beloved. The result, however, is abject failure. Attraction is not 'negotiable': there is nothing the male suitor can offer that will convince the female to relent when the female does not experience desire naturally. Olivia can freely recognise Orsino's objective merits but still she does not love.

So what does inspire love? Nature and instinct, first of all: as in several of his other tales, Shakespeare's characters fall fast and they fall hard—usually at first sight and often in opposition to social convention. Attraction in *Twelfth Night* is intensified by barriers and by difficulty: Orsino pursues the unyielding Olivia; Olivia is thunderstruck by the resistant Cesario (actually Viola); and Viola falls for her master Orsino while disguised as a boy in his service. If it is a general truth that we undervalue what comes easily and overvalue what comes only with difficulty, this is especially true when it comes to attraction. Olivia is a case in point: she is totally underawed by the compliments and professions of love from Orsino, and responds by listing her physical features as if they were mere chattels of no particular value. When Cesario (Viola) rejects her, on the other hand, and especially when he (she) insults her, Olivia is attracted and intrigued. All are seeking partners of higher value than themselves, but since value cannot be perceived directly, it can only be inferred from behaviour, and the behaviour that most clearly appears to demonstrate higher value is disinterest and disregard.

The prose version of the tale excludes one of the more memorable figures from Shakespeare's original—Olivia's steward, Malvolio. Malvolio is the great 'denier': he is a puritan and a killjoy who adopts a manner of high-handed moral superiority over the other characters of the play. But he is also a great hypocrite who himself seeks to take advantage of his position to obtain his lady's love and the benefits that go with it. Shakespeare concludes with this figure being thoroughly mocked and ultimately removed from the world that remains to be inhabited by more cheerful, if less censorious, characters. Whatever absurdities our natural instincts might lead us into, Shakespeare seems to say, it is infinitely preferable to follow those instincts than it is to subject ourselves to hypocritical and self-serving arbitrators of decency. After all: who judges the judges? Let there be, then, says Sir Toby Belch (on behalf, no doubt, of Shakespeare) 'cakes and ale'.

TWELFTH NIGHT

Sebastian and his sister Viola, a young gentleman and lady of Messaline, were twins, and (which was accounted a great wonder) from their birth they so much resembled each other that, but for the difference in their dress, they could not be known apart. They were both born in one hour, and in one hour they were both in danger of perishing, for they were shipwrecked on the coast of Illyria as they were making a sea voyage together. The ship, on board of which they were, split on a rock in a violent storm, and a very small number of the ship's company escaped with their lives. The captain of the vessel, with a few of the sailors that were saved, got to land in a small boat, and with them they brought Viola safe on shore, where she, poor lady, instead of rejoicing at her own deliverance, began to lament her brother's loss; but the captain comforted her with the assurance that he had seen her brother, when the ship split, fasten himself to a strong mast, on which, as long as he could see anything of him for the distance, he perceived him borne up above the waves. Viola was much consoled by the hope this account gave her, and now considered how she was to dispose of herself in a strange country, so far from home; and she asked the captain if he knew anything of Illyria. 'Ay, very well, madam,' replied the captain, 'for I was born not three hours' travel from this place.' 'Who governs here?' said Viola. The captain told her, Illyria was governed by Orsino, a duke noble in nature as well as dignity. Viola said she had heard her father speak of Orsino, and that he was unmarried then. 'And he is so now,' said the captain, 'or was so very lately, for, but a month ago, I went from here, and then it was the general talk (as you know what great ones do, the people will prattle of) that Orsino sought the love of fair Olivia, a virtuous maid, the daughter of a count who died twelve months ago, leaving Olivia to the protection of her brother, who shortly after died also; and for the love of this dear brother, they say, she has abjured the sight and company of men.' Viola, who was herself in such a sad affliction for her brother's loss, wished she could live with this lady, who so tenderly mourned a brother's death. She asked the captain if he could introduce her to Olivia, saying she would willingly serve this lady. But he replied this would be a hard thing to accomplish, because the lady Olivia would admit no person into her house since her brother's death, not even the Duke himself. Then Viola formed another project in her mind, which was, in a man's habit, to serve the Duke Orsino as a page. It was a strange fancy in a young lady to put on male attire, and pass for a boy; but the forlorn and unprotected state of Viola, who was young and of uncommon beauty, alone, and in a foreign land, must plead her excuse.

She having observed a fair behaviour in the captain, and that he showed a friendly concern for her welfare, entrusted him with her design, and he readily engaged to assist her. Viola gave him money, and directed him to furnish her with suitable apparel, ordering her clothes to be made of the same colour and in the same fashion her brother Sebastian used to wear, and when she was dressed in her manly garb, she looked so exactly like her brother that some strange errors happened by means of their being mistaken for each other; for, as will afterwards appear, Sebastian was also saved.

Viola's good friend, the captain, when he had transformed this pretty lady into a gentleman, having some interest at court, got her presented to Orsino under the feigned name of Cesario. The Duke was wonderfully pleased with the address and graceful deportment of this handsome youth, and made Cesario one of his pages, that being the office Viola wished to obtain; and she so well fulfilled the duties of her new station, and showed such a ready observance and faithful attachment to her lord, that she soon became his most favoured attendant. To Cesario Orsino confided the whole history of his love for the lady Olivia. To Cesario he told the long and unsuccessful suit he had made to one who, rejecting his long services, and despising his person, refused to admit him to her presence; and for the love of this lady who had so unkindly treated him, the noble Orsino, forsaking the sports of the field and all manly exercises in which he used to delight, passed his hours in ignoble sloth, listening to the effeminate sounds of soft music, gentle airs, and passionate love songs; and neglecting the company of the wise and learned lords with whom he used to associate, he was now all day long conversing with young Cesario. Unmeet companion no doubt his grave courtiers thought Cesario was for their once noble master, the great Duke Orsino.

It is a dangerous matter for young maidens to be the confidants of handsome young dukes; which Viola too soon found to her sorrow, for all that Orsino told her he endured for Olivia, she presently perceived she suffered for the love of him; and much it moved her wonder that Olivia could be so regardless of this her peerless lord and master, whom she thought no one could behold without the deepest admiration, and she ventured gently to hint to Orsino that it was a pity he should affect a lady who was so blind to his worthy qualities; and she said: 'If a lady were to love you, my lord, as you love Olivia (and perhaps there may be one who does), if you could not love her in return, would you not tell her that you could not love, and must she not be content with this answer?' But Orsino would not admit of this reasoning, for he denied that it was possible for any woman to love as he did. He said no woman's heart was big enough to hold so much love, and therefore it was unfair to compare the love of any lady for him to his love for Olivia. Now, though Viola had the utmost deference for the Duke's opinions, she could not help thinking this was not quite true, for she thought her heart had full as much love in it as Orsino's had; and she said: 'Ah, but I know, my lord.' 'What do you know, Cesario?' said Orsino. 'Too well I know,' replied Viola, 'what love women may owe to men. They are as true of heart as we are. My father had a daughter loved a man, as I perhaps, were I a woman, should love your lordship.' 'And what is her history?' said Orsino. 'A blank, my lord,' replied Viola. 'She never told her love, but let concealment, like a worm in the bud, feed on her damask cheek. She pined in thought, and with a green and yellow melancholy, she sat like Patience on a monument, smiling at Grief.' The Duke inquired if this lady died of her love, but to this question Viola returned an evasive answer; as probably she had feigned the story, to speak words expressive of the secret love and silent grief she suffered for Orsino.

While they were talking, a gentleman entered whom the Duke had sent to Olivia, and he said: 'So please you, my lord, I might not be admitted to the lady, but by her handmaid she returned you this answer: Until seven years hence, the element itself shall not behold her face; but like a cloistress she will walk veiled, watering her chamber with her tears for the sad remembrance of her dead brother.' On hearing this, the Duke exclaimed: 'O she that has a heart of this fine frame to pay this debt of love to a dead brother, how will she love when the rich golden shaft has touched her heart!' And then he said to Viola: 'You know, Cesario, I have told you all the secrets of my heart; therefore, good youth, go to Olivia's house. Be not denied access; stand at her doors, and tell her, there your fixed foot shall grow till you have audience.' 'And if I do speak to her, my lord, what then?' said Viola. 'O then,' replied Orsino, 'unfold to her the passion of my love. Make a long discourse to her of my dear faith. It will well become you to act my woes, for she will attend more to you than to one of graver aspect.'

Away then went Viola; but not willingly did she undertake this courtship, for she was to woo a lady to become a wife to him she wished to marry; but having undertaken the affair, she performed it with

242

fidelity; and Olivia soon heard that a youth was at her door who insisted upon being admitted to her presence. 'I told him,' said the servant, 'that you were sick: he said he knew you were, and therefore he came to speak with you. I told him that you were asleep: he seemed to have a foreknowledge of that too, and said, that therefore he must speak with you. What is to be said to him, lady? For he seems fortified against all denial, and will speak with you, whether you will or no.' Olivia, curious to see who this peremptory messenger might be, desired he might be admitted; and throwing her veil over her face, she said she would once more hear Orsino's embassy, not doubting but that he came from the Duke, by his importunity. Viola, entering, put on the most manly air she could assume, and affecting the fine courtier language of great men's pages, she said to the veiled lady: 'Most radiant, exquisite, and matchless beauty, I pray you tell me if you are the lady of the house; for I should be sorry to cast away my speech upon another; for besides that it is excellently well penned, I have taken great pains to learn it.' 'Whence come you, sir?' said Olivia. 'I can say little more than I have studied,' replied Viola, 'and that question is out of my part.' 'Are you a comedian?' said Olivia. 'No,' replied Viola, 'and yet I am not that which I play'; meaning that she, being a woman, feigned herself to be a man. And again she asked Olivia if she were the lady of the house. Olivia said she was; and then Viola, having more curiosity to see her rival's features than haste to deliver her master's message, said: 'Good madam, let me see your face.' With this bold request Olivia was not averse to comply; for this haughty beauty, whom the Duke Orsino had loved so long in vain, at first sight conceived a passion for the supposed page, the humble Cesario.

When Viola asked to see her face, Olivia said: 'Have you any commission from your lord and master to negotiate with my face?' And then, forgetting her determination to go veiled for seven long years, she drew aside her veil, saying: 'But I will draw the curtain and show the picture. Is it not well done?'

Viola replied: 'It is beauty truly mixed; the red and white upon your cheeks is by Nature's own cunning hand laid on. You are the most cruel lady living, if you will lead these graces to the grave, and leave the world no copy.' 'O, sir,' replied Olivia, 'I will not be so

cruel. The world may have an inventory of my beauty.
As, item, two lips, indifferent red; item, two grey eyes,
with lids to them; one neck; one chin; and so forth.
Were you sent here to praise me?' Viola replied: 'I see
what you are: you are too proud, but you are fair. My
lord and master loves you. O such a love could but be
recompensed, though you were crowned the queen
of beauty: for Orsino loves you with adoration and
with tears, with groans that thunder love, and sighs
of fire.' 'Your lord,' said Olivia, 'knows well my mind.
I cannot love him; yet I doubt not he is virtuous; I
know him to be noble and of high estate, of fresh
and spotless youth. All voices proclaim him learned,
courteous, and valiant; yet I cannot love him, he
might have taken his answer long ago.' 'If I did love
you as my master does,' said Viola, 'I would make
me a willow cabin at your gates, and call upon your
name, I would write complaining sonnets on Olivia,
and sing them in the dead of the night; your name
should sound among the hills, and I would make
Echo, the babbling gossip of the air, cry out Olivia.
O you should not rest between the elements of earth
and air, but you should pity me. 'You might do much,'
said Olivia. 'What is your parentage?' Viola replied:
'Above my fortunes, yet my state is well. I am a
gentleman.' Olivia now reluctantly dismissed Viola,
saying: 'Go to your master, and tell him I cannot love
him. Let him send no more, unless perchance you
come again to tell me how he takes it.' And Viola
departed, bidding the lady farewell by the name of

Fair Cruelty. When she was gone, Olivia repeated the words, 'Above my fortunes, yet my state is well. I am a gentleman.' And she said aloud: 'I will be sworn he is; his tongue, his face, his limbs, action, and spirit, plainly show he is a gentleman.' And then she wished Cesario was the Duke; and perceiving the fast hold he had taken on her affections, she blamed herself for her sudden love: but the gentle blame which people lay upon their own faults has no deep root; and presently the noble lady Olivia so far forgot the inequality between her fortunes and those of this seeming page, as well as the maidenly reserve which is the chief ornament of a lady's character, that she resolved to court the love of young Cesario, and sent a servant after him with a diamond ring, under the pretence that he had left it with her as a present from Orsino. She hoped by thus artfully making Cesario a present of the ring, she should give him some intimation of her design; and truly it did make Viola suspect; for knowing that Orsino had sent no ring by her, she began to recollect that Olivia's looks and manner were expressive of admiration, and she presently guessed her master's mistress had fallen in love with her. 'Alas,' said she, 'the poor lady might as well love a dream. Disguise I see is wicked, for it has caused Olivia to breathe as fruitless sighs for me as I do for Orsino.'

Viola returned to Orsino's palace, and related to her lord the ill success of the negotiation, repeating the command of Olivia that the Duke should trouble her no more. Yet still the Duke persisted in hoping that the gentle Cesario would in time be able to persuade her to show some pity, and therefore he bade him he should go to her again the next day. In the meantime, to pass away the tedious interval, he commanded a song which he loved to be sung; and he said: 'My good Cesario, when I heard that song last night, methought it did relieve my passion much. Mark it, Cesario, it is old and plain. The spinsters and the knitters when they sit in the sun, and the young maids that weave their thread with bone, chant this song. It is silly, yet I love it, for it tells of the innocence of love in the old times.'

SONG

Come away, come away, Death,
And in sad cypress let me be laid;
Fly away, fly away, breath,
I am slain by a fair cruel maid.
My shroud of white stuck all with yew, O prepare it!
My part of death no one so true did share it.

Not a flower, not a flower sweet,
On my black coffin let there be strewn:
Not a friend, not a friend greet
My poor corpse, where my bones shall be thrown.
A thousand thousand sighs to save, lay me O where
Sad true lover never find my grave, to weep there!

Viola did not fail to mark the words of the old song,

which in such true simplicity described the pangs of unrequited love, and she bore testimony in her countenance of feeling what the song expressed. Her sad looks were observed by Orsino, who said to her: 'My life upon it, Cesario, though you are so young, your eye has looked upon some face that it loves: has it not, boy?' 'A little, with your leave,' replied Viola. 'And what kind of woman, and of what age is she?' said Orsino. 'Of your age and of your complexion, my lord,' said Viola; which made the Duke smile to hear this fair young boy loved a woman so much older than himself, and of a man's dark complexion; but Viola secretly meant Orsino, and not a woman like him.

When Viola made her second visit to Olivia, she found no difficulty in gaining access to her. Servants soon discover when their ladies delight to converse with handsome young messengers; and the instant Viola arrived, the gates were thrown wide open, and the Duke's page was shown into Olivia's apartment with great respect; and when Viola told Olivia that she was come once more to plead in her lord's behalf, this lady said: 'I desired you never to speak of him again; but if you would undertake another suit, I had rather hear you solicit, than music from the spheres.' This was pretty plain speaking, but Olivia soon explained herself still more plainly, and openly confessed her love; and when she saw displeasure with perplexity expressed in Viola's face, she said: 'O what a deal of scorn looks beautiful in the contempt and anger of his lip! Cesario, by the roses of the spring, by maidhood, honour, and by truth, I love you so, that, in spite of your pride, I have neither wit nor reason to conceal my passion.'

But in vain the lady wooed; Viola hastened from her presence, threatening never more to come to plead Orsino's love; and all the reply she made to Olivia's fond solicitation was a declaration of a resolution never to love any woman.

No sooner had Viola left the lady than a claim was made upon her valour. A gentleman, a rejected suitor of Olivia, who had learned how that lady had favoured the Duke's messenger, challenged him to fight a duel. What should poor Viola do, who, though she carried a manlike outside, had a true woman's heart, and feared to look on her own sword?

When she saw her formidable rival advancing towards her with his sword drawn, she began to think of confessing that she was a woman; but she was relieved at once from her terror, and the shame of such a discovery, by a stranger that was passing by, who made up to them, and as if he had been long known to her, and were her dearest friend, said to her opponent: 'If this young gentleman has done offence, I will take the fault on me; and if you offend him, I will for his sake defy you.' Before Viola had time to thank him for his protection, or to inquire the reason of his kind interference, her new friend met with an enemy where his bravery was of no use to him; for the officers of justice coming up in that instant, apprehended the stranger in the Duke's name to answer for an offence he had committed some years before; and he said to Viola: 'This comes with seeking you'; and then he asked her for a purse, saying: 'Now my necessity makes me ask for my purse, and it grieves me much more for what I cannot do for you than for what befalls myself. You stand amazed, but be of comfort.' His words did indeed amaze Viola, and she protested she knew him not, nor had ever received a purse from him; but for the kindness he had just shown her, she offered him a small sum of money, being nearly the whole she possessed. And now the stranger spoke severe things, charging her with ingratitude and unkindness. He said: 'This youth, whom you see here, I snatched from the jaws of death and for his sake alone I came to Illyria, and have fallen into this danger.' But the officers cared little for hearkening to the complaints of their prisoner, and they hurried him off, saying: 'What is that to us?' And as he was carried away he called Viola by the name of Sebastian, reproaching the supposed Sebastian for disowning his friend, as long as he was within hearing. When Viola heard herself called Sebastian, though the stranger was taken away too hastily for her to ask an explanation, she conjectured that this seeming mystery might arise from her being mistaken for her brother; and she began to cherish hopes that it was her brother whose life this man said he had preserved. And so indeed it was. The stranger, whose name was Antonio, was a sea-captain. He had taken Sebastian up into his ship when, almost exhausted with fatigue, he was floating on the mast to which he had fastened himself in the storm. Antonio conceived such a friendship for Sebastian that he resolved to accompany him whithersoever he went; and when the youth expressed a curiosity to visit

Orsino's court, Antonio, rather than part from him, came to Illyria, though he knew, if his person should be known there, his life would be in danger, because in a sea-fight he had once dangerously wounded the Duke Orsino's nephew. This was the offence for which he was now made a prisoner.

Antonio and Sebastian had landed together but a few hours before Antonio met Viola. He had given his purse to Sebastian, desiring him to use it freely if he saw anything he wished to purchase, telling him he would wait at the inn while Sebastian went to view the town; but Sebastian not returning at the time appointed, Antonio had ventured out to look for him, and Viola being dressed the same, and in face so exactly resembling her brother, Antonio drew his sword (as he thought) in defence of the youth he had saved, and when Sebastian (as he supposed)

disowned him and denied him his own purse, no
wonder he accused him of ingratitude.

Viola, when Antonio was gone, fearing a second
invitation to fight, slunk home as fast as she could.
She had not been long gone, when her adversary
thought he saw her return; but it was her brother
Sebastian, who happened to arrive at this place, and
he said: 'Now, sir, have I met with you again? There's
for you'; and struck him a blow. Sebastian was no
coward; he returned the blow with interest, and drew
his sword.

A lady now put a stop to this duel, for Olivia came
out of the house, and she too mistaking Sebastian
for Cesario, invited him to come into her house,
expressing much sorrow at the rude attack he had
met with. Though Sebastian was as much surprised
at the courtesy of this lady as at the rudeness of his
unknown foe, yet he went very willingly into the
house, and Olivia was delighted to find Cesario (as
she thought him) become more sensible of her
attentions; for though their features were exactly the
same, there was none of the contempt and anger to be
seen in his face, which she had complained of when
she told her love to Cesario.

Sebastian did not at all object to the fondness the
lady lavished on him. He seemed to take it in very
good part, yet he wondered how it had come to pass,
and he was rather inclined to think Olivia was not in
her right senses; but perceiving that she was mistress
of a fine house, and that she ordered her affairs and

seemed to govern her family discreetly, and that in all but her sudden love for him she appeared in the full possession of her reason, he well approved of the courtship; and Olivia finding Cesario in this good humour, and fearing he might change his mind, proposed that, as she had a priest in the house, they should be instantly married. Sebastian assented to this proposal; and when the marriage ceremony was over, he left his lady for a short time, intending to go and tell his friend Antonio the good fortune that he had met with. In the meantime Orsino came to visit Olivia; and at the moment he arrived before Olivia's house, the officers of justice brought their prisoner, Antonio, before the Duke. Viola was with Orsino, her master; and when Antonio saw Viola, whom he still imagined to be Sebastian, he told the Duke in what manner he had rescued this youth from the perils of the sea; and after fully relating all the kindness he had really shown to Sebastian, he ended his complaint with saying that for three months, both day and night, this ungrateful youth had been with him. But now the lady Olivia coming forth from her house, the Duke could no longer attend to Antonio's story; and he said: 'Here comes the countess: now Heaven walks on earth! But for thee, fellow, thy words are madness. Three months has this youth attended on me'; and then he ordered Antonio to be taken aside. But Orsino's heavenly countess soon gave the Duke cause to accuse Cesario as much of ingratitude as Antonio had done, for all the words he could hear

Olivia speak were words of kindness to Cesario; and when he found his page had obtained this high place in Olivia's favour, he threatened him with all the terrors of his just revenge; and as he was going to depart, he called Viola to follow him, saying: 'Come, boy, with me. My thoughts are ripe for mischief.' Though it seemed in his jealous rage he was going to doom Viola to instant death, yet her love made her no longer a coward, and she said she would most joyfully suffer death to give her master ease. But Olivia would not so lose her husband, and she cried: 'Where goes my Cesario?' Viola replied: 'After him I love more than my life.' Olivia, however, prevented their departure by loudly proclaiming that Cesario was her husband, and sent for the priest, who declared that not two hours had passed since he had married the Lady Olivia to this young man. In vain Viola protested she was not married to Olivia; the evidence of that lady and the priest made Orsino believe that his page had robbed him of the treasure he prized above his life. But thinking that it was past recall, he was bidding farewell to his faithless mistress, and the young dissembler, her husband, as he called Viola, warning her never to come in his sight again, when (as it seemed to them) a miracle appeared! For another Cesario entered, and addressed Olivia as his wife. This new Cesario was Sebastian, the real husband of Olivia; and when their wonder had a little ceased at seeing two persons with the same face, the same voice, and the same habit, the brother and sister began to question each other; for Viola could scarce be persuaded that her brother was living, and Sebastian knew not how to account for the sister he supposed drowned being found in the habit of a young man. But Viola presently acknowledged that she was indeed Viola, and his sister, under that disguise.

When all the errors were cleared up which the extreme likeness between this twin brother and sister had occasioned, they laughed at the Lady Olivia for the pleasant mistake she had made in falling in love with a woman; and Olivia showed no dislike to her exchange, when she found she had wedded the brother instead of the sister.

The hopes of Orsino were for ever at an end by this marriage of Olivia, and with his hopes, all his fruitless love seemed to vanish away, and all his thoughts were fixed on the event of his favourite, young Cesario, being changed into a fair lady. He viewed Viola with great attention, and he remembered how very handsome he had always thought Cesario was, and he concluded she would look very beautiful in a woman's attire; and then he remembered how often she had said she loved him, which at the time seemed only the dutiful expressions of a faithful page; but now he guessed that something more was meant, for many of her pretty sayings, which were like riddles to him, came now into his mind, and he no sooner remembered all these things than he resolved to make Viola his wife; and he said to her (he still could not help calling her Cesario and boy): 'Boy, you have said to me a thousand times that you should never love a woman like to me, and for the faithful service you have done for me so much beneath your soft and tender breeding, and since you have called me master so long, you shall now be your master's mistress, and Orsino's true Duchess.'

Olivia, perceiving Orsino was making over that heart, which she had so ungraciously rejected, to Viola, invited them to enter her house, and offered the assistance of the good priest who had married her to Sebastian in the morning, to perform the same ceremony in the remaining part of the day for Orsino and Viola. Thus the twin brother and sister were both wedded on the same day: the storm and shipwreck, which had separated them, being the means of bringing to pass their high and mighty fortunes. Viola was the wife of Orsino, the Duke of Illyria, and Sebastian the husband of the rich and noble countess, the Lady Olivia.

RESOURCES

Shakespeare Editions
For the complete works, the Oxford, Norton, and Riverside editions can all be recommended. For individual plays, as a general rule the Arden editions are excellent.

Shakespeare on Screen
There are cinematic versions of many of Shakespeare's plays, some of them excellent. The BBC have filmed all the plays for television as 'The Shakespeare Collection'.

Further Information and Resources
Further information on recommended texts, cinematic versions, and suggested reading can be found at www.andrewlynn.com.

Made in the USA
Lexington, KY
29 November 2018